Robert L. Maddox

PROSTATE CANCER

What I Found Out & What You Should Know

Harold Shaw Publishers
Wheaton, Illinois

All Scripture quotations, unless otherwise indicated, are taken from the HOLY BIBLE, NEW INTERNATIONAL VERSION®. NIV® Copyright © 1973, 1978, 1984 International Bible Society. Used by permission of Zondervan Publishing House. All rights reserved.

ISBN 0-87788-566-4

Edited by Robert Bittner and Miriam Mindeman

Cover design by David LaPlaca

Library of Congress Cataloging-in-Publication Data

Maddox, Robert L.
    Prostate cancer : what I found out, and what you should know / by Robert L. Maddox ; foreword by retired Senator Robert Dole.
       p. cm.
    ISBN 0-87788-566-4
    1. Maddox, Robert L.—Health. 2. Prostate—Cancer—Patients—United States—Biography. I. Title.
    RC280.P7M3 1997
    362.1'9699463—dc21
    [b]
                                      97-20186
                                      CIP

02 01 00 99 98 97

10 9 8 7 6 5 4 3 2 1

Dedicated to the loving memory of
Robert L. Maddox, Sr.
and
H. Burton Foster

And with sincere appreciation for valuable assistance
from the Foster family;
the Cancer Research Foundation of America,
Bo Aldige, executive director;
and Dr. James B. Regan
and the staff of Georgetown University Medical Center,
Washington, D.C.

Contents

Foreword

I may have lost an election in 1996, but several years ago I won a much more important battle against prostate cancer. Early detection was the key to my victory—and it was the key to the victory that Bob Maddox details in this personal and inspirational book.

Bob has written about his bout with prostate cancer in a warm, humorous, readable, and reliable style. His experiences with hospital routine, surgery, and recuperation can give heart and hope to a person facing any sort of serious illness—and especially men dealing with prostate cancer.

I urge you to read this book—and, more importantly—I join Bob Maddox in urging men to see their doctors often and to be tested for any sign of prostate cancer. It saved my life. It just might save yours.

Robert J. Dole
U.S. Senator (retired)

Chapter 1

Setting the Stage

What happens to a man, his wife, and his family when the doctor announces, "You have prostate cancer"? What kind of medical minuet begins to swirl when treatment for the malady gets under way? What is left of a man, his sexual capacity, even his ability to control his bladder, when the cancer industry gets through with him?

I can speak from experience about all of these questions.

Though nothing new, prostate cancer has come out of the closet, bringing with it the revelation that millions of men have some form of prostate problem. Over 300,000 men each year face the specter of full-blown cancer. To make matters even more severe, agencies tracking prostate cancer estimate that approximately 40,000 men a year die from the disease.

The list of recent victims reads like a virtual Who's Who of contemporary life: Laurence Olivier, Bill Bixby, Telly Savalas, Don Ameche, James Herriott, Frank Zappa, Senator Spark Matsunaga, Frank Perry, L. D. Johnson, Bobby Riggs, and François Mitterrand, to name a few. The list of those who have eluded the cancer's fatal clutches likewise embraces some of our best-known figures: Senator Robert Dole, Senator Ted Stevens, Senator Paul Sarbanes, General Norman Schwarzkopf, Secretary of Education James Riley, U.S. House of Representatives Chaplain James Ford, Justice John Paul Stevens, Jerry Lewis, Michael Milken, and Harry Belafonte.

It happened to me. It really did. Out of the blue—with no warning shots across the bow of my life—the doctor said, "You've got it. You've got prostate cancer."

I did not breathe for a couple of seconds. Then, after my vision cleared and my heart pumped again, I realized I had to get on with this chapter and the rest of my life. And I have.

Expanding waves of publicity about prostate cancer and the early death of my own father had prompted me to drop by the doctor's office one day for a routine checkup. Within a few weeks I was lying on an operating table. Within a few months I could continue my life, distinctly altered, but with an almost zero fear of that cancer's recurrence. (Some other form of the dread condition may rise up and strike me, but I can live 99 percent free from prostate-cancer concerns.)

A Word of Introduction

Since you and I will be spending some time together—and sharing details that are about as intimate as they can get—it might be helpful for you to know something about me. Me as a person, that is, and not just a medical procedure.

At a young age, I responded to a sense of call to the ministry (in my case, within the Baptist tradition). In the 1970s I began writing professionally while serving as a Georgia county-seat town pastor. Through a series of serendipitous connections, I came to know Jimmy and Rosalynn Carter, some of their family, and Jody and Nan Powell. In the early days of the Carter presidency, Jody, President Carter's press secretary, and members of Mrs. Carter's staff would sometimes call me for ideas about specific White House speeches dealing with religious and family issues. Mrs. Carter even asked me to help her with an event that resulted in an unforgettable 1978 Thanksgiving holiday in the White House for my wife, Linda, and me. In 1979 the Carters invited me to join the White House staff as a speech writer and, subsequently, to take up the exciting, if daunting, task of interpreting the president to the religious community—especially the increasingly politically focused Christian conservatives.

> **The cancer became a gathering-up experience that continues to shape my life.**

After Carter's defeat in 1980, my family and I took up a nomadic existence until the spring of 1984, when I moved back to Washington to become executive director of Americans United for Separation of Church and State, a well-respected religious liberty organization. During those extraordinary public years I had great fun appearing on practically every national radio and television show, including an early version of the *Larry King Live* program.

In the spring of 1992, I returned to professional ministry and took up duties as pastor of Briggs Memorial Baptist Church in suburban Washington, D.C.

My bout with prostate cancer began two years later.

The cancer became a gathering-up experience that continues to shape my life and the life of my family. This book grows out of that cluster of life episodes. We are not done with the shaping yet. In fact, I expect the reshaping and reforming will continue until some other condition or situation "gathers me to my fathers."

Why This Book?

I write this book because I like to write, because writing it has helped me get many aspects of life in better perspective, and because I want to help others have a better shake at their "three score and ten."

An operation for cancer, albeit quite serious, is a kaleidoscopic experience. By being personal, candid, and informative, I hope to make it easier for other men to deal forthrightly with their own fears and ambiguous feelings. Cancer is certainly nothing to laugh at—but in the course of confronting it, family, friends, and I did laugh. We had to. It served to relieve the anxiety, even terror I felt at times. And I am not alone. My experiences have resonated with other men when we have compared notes and showed our scars.

This book comes with hope and assurance that a bout with prostate cancer need not be disabling, especially if it is discovered early. I would hope that my cancer story, research, and life journey will serve as a strong kick in the pants to other guys to get their prostate glands checked every now and then—especially after you hit the forty-year mark. If there is a problem—and you will not know without an examination—chances are good you can head it off. Stop it in its tracks. Taking responsibility for your own health must be uppermost in your mind. Procrastination, denial, and undue dependence on the family doctor can spell big trouble.

Grounded in Faith

Though I will expand on my theology along the way, I say up front that I believe in God. Providence. The Work of the Spirit. The Whisper in the Night. The Bright Hope Offered by Tomorrow's Dawn. And in the worst of times, maybe even the Tooth Fairy.

For most of my life, a working faith has been my primary reference point to such a degree that I would hate to face an episode of cancer without it. I could not possibly undertake a book like this without seeing the whole episode through my relationship with God. It comes down to faith: faith in God's willingness to remain involved in the basic stuff of my existence and faith in his ability to turn most of my NOes into resounding YESes. This is what provides the ground of being for me. About the time I think I have the Lord figured out, some new wrinkle pushes me to take yet another quantum leap with him.

> **For most of my life, a working faith has been my primary reference point.**

This book, then, has become part of another of those awesome, numbing yet invigorating leaps forward. I surely do welcome the chance to have you leap with me as we help men and their families deal with a serious but manageable problem.

What happened to me has also set me on my own charging white horse running up and down the roads of the nation alerting other men to the dangers of neglect. Not content, however, only to ring the bell of alarm, I want to point the afflicted ones, especially those with cancer, to wholeness and hope. At this writing, I am not there yet. I am not sure where "there" is, but I have not made it. Nevertheless, I am on my way.

You, be you male (young or old) or female (wife, lover, mother, sister, or daughter), should read this book because it deals with a major killer of American men—men, like my father, who could have enjoyed much longer lives, if only they had faced the possibility of prostate cancer earlier.

Chapter 2

Saved by the Trees

Who would have thought that a few ordinary, garden-variety pine trees growing in a sandy yard in Florida's Panhandle would save my life? But that is exactly what happened.

In late 1969, my parents, Bob and Virginia Maddox, found *The Cottage*. While aimlessly driving through Panama City Beach, Florida, on a quick fishing trip, they came upon a little hull of a house about three hundred yards from the beach on a short side street. Judging from the tattered appearance, someone obviously had begun construction, then abandoned the job, leaving only the concrete slab floor, concrete block walls, and roof. The shell contained no windows or doors, and nothing inside other than the earliest stages of roughed-in rooms. Something about the forlorn, weather-worn cottage on a bare, sandy lot in the low-rent section of the beach community appealed to my father. Too busy with graduate school and rearing my own children to ask much about his latest project, I hardly remember the actual purchase. I do recall his proud announcement that he and Mother planned to buy the place and fix it up.

It was a good time in their lives. Long a leader in the

local Baptist church, my father had expanded his Christian witness to become an active member of Gideon's International, the lay organization that promotes Bible distribution. Daddy loved traveling around to various churches talking about the importance of the Bible in people's lives and promoting the work of the Gideons.

In addition, he had a flourishing business as a representative for a commercial janitorial supply company. His four sons were finally through college, and he and Mother had managed to pull together enough money to become partners in a proposed Holiday Inn in Bainbridge, Georgia, in the late 1960s. He had also become the catalyst for the construction of a nursing home in their town of Thomaston, Georgia. As was frequently the case, short on funds but long on energy and imagination, he put the deals together and received a portion of the ownership in exchange for his efforts. A cottage at the beach? Why not? He and Mother, the four of us brothers, and our expanding families could congregate at the seashore and have a good time together. Like a proud lord of the manor, Daddy no doubt envisioned himself gathering his brood around him, basking in the glow of their accomplishments, warmed by their love and admiration.

Within a short time he and Mother had purchased the house and lot for less than five thousand dollars, money he borrowed from one of his many banker friends, who loaned him what he needed—not on the property, but on his signature. He found a local carpenter down on his luck who agreed to finish the house inside. For very little money he built out the inner space of the cottage into three small bedrooms, a larger kitchen, dining and living areas, and a "Florida room" that soon became a fourth bedroom. Though Father could do almost any kind of work himself, and wanted to, Mother persuaded him to concentrate on his selling and deals, letting the carpenter do the manual labor. Still, he and Mother regularly made the five-hour run from Thomaston to check on the cottage. The two of them painted the outside block walls white and eventually put up some aluminum awnings. In a flash of inspiration and energy, Daddy stuck a screened porch on the front of the house, not his finest piece of carpentry.

In the summer of 1970, my family and I made our first trek to the cottage, driving down from Atlanta where I was in graduate school at Emory University's Candler School of Theology. I had not seen the house in its raw state and could not sufficiently appreciate the miracle Bob, Virginia, and the rather hapless carpenter had wrought. To our pleasant surprise, we walked into a neat little cottage finished with pecan paneling and burnt orange carpet. Thereafter, we made regular trips to the cottage, going nearly every year for at least a brief stay.

As much as he loved the cottage, Daddy did not like to sit on the beach or swim in the ocean. He did like for us to come and indulge our fancies. If he and Mother happened to be at the house with us, he would get peeved if I did not spend some time helping him work on the place. I felt torn between wanting to spend all the time I could with my wife, Linda, and the children, and helping him with repairs and projects. Now that I own the place I can understand his feelings.

At some point, probably in the fall of 1971, he set out some trees in the front yard. Nothing exotic, mainly eight or ten pine trees. He also found a bargain in full-grown palm trees and had four of them hauled in and planted across the front of the yard, right at the street. One of the palms soon died, though the naked trunk housed birds for several seasons before a strong wind finally toppled it. The rest of the palms have survived along with the pine trees. Daddy also sprigged the yard with St. Augustine grass, a species that grows well in sandy soil. Despite rather monumental neglect, the grass has hung on and made the yard look rather decent. He put out some holly bushes and Kmart shrubs, some of which have also survived despite the ravages of grandchildren, insects, and time.

During an especially hectic period in our lives, I missed going to the cottage for about three years, though Linda and the children went. When I did get to go back, the place looked different. At first I could not decide what had created the change. Then it dawned on me: the pine trees. They had really grown up. When last I noticed them, they were just scrubs. Now they reached above the house, providing soft, pine-needle-sighing shade for the front

> **How Daddy would have loved to see his trees all grown up.**

of the house. Amazing, those trees. How they had grown. And how Daddy would have loved to see his trees all grown up. But he did not live to see the fruits of his labor.

A Lump Found and Forgotten

About the time he bought the cottage, Daddy wanted to secure additional life insurance. At his age—something like fifty-eight or fifty-nine—he was required by the insurance company to have a cursory physical examination before being issued the policy. In the examination, the hometown doctor, his good friend, found a lump on his prostate gland.

"Bob," the doctor said, "you need to keep a close eye on that knot on your prostate. I don't believe it's a problem right now. But in three months, you should let the urologist examine you."

Well, never one for doctors anyway, and being very busy—and literally having the time of his life as a top salesman, prime mover for the development of the new Holiday Inn and nursing home, and now proud owner of a house at the beach—Daddy forgot or ignored the doctor's advice. Besides, he had none of the signs of that "old man's ailment," prostate trouble. He could urinate when necessary. He and Mother were completely happy—including sexually, I suppose, though they never discussed that part of their lives with any of us. No problem, not to worry! He certainly had no time to interrupt his life to see a doctor.

A couple of years later, Dr. Tyler and Mother encountered each other in the post office. Their physician friend asked, "Virginia, did Bob ever have that lump on his prostate checked? I haven't seen him since I found it."

Mother vaguely remembered hearing Daddy mention Dr. Tyler's admonition, but it had not seriously registered with her. Immediately, however, she made Daddy go back for another checkup. After a quick examination, the doctor became alarmed and sent my father to the urologist, who promptly placed him in the hospital for further testing. An operation confirmed Dr. Bruton's fears.

"Bob," he said, while Mother and my wife stood at the bedside, "you have a fairly serious cancer situation. The malignancy has spread too far to make removal of the prostate possible. I did all I could, but you will have to undergo further treatment. I don't believe the prostate cancer will take your life, but you will have to deal with it."

Cancer Takes Its Toll

That was the early 1970s—generations, medically speaking, from where we are today. Because of my father's neglect, his cancer condition had spread beyond the prostate gland, invading other adjacent organs. Dr. Bruton, using a perineal approach (coming in between the rectum and scrotum) in vogue in those days, removed all the infected tissue he could, but he simply could not do sufficient cutting to remove all the damage. Following the surgery, Daddy would have six weeks of radiation therapy. His particular condition made it necessary for him to go to the Medical College of Georgia in Augusta for this protocol.

> **The early 1970s was, medically speaking, generations away from where we are now.**

I can still remember him laughing and teasing about crawling up on the cold, hard table and tugging at the skimpy hospital gown, trying to keep some of the more private parts of his battered body covered, as if the radiation technicians cared what he bared.

He was able to keep running his business from home. He and Mother squeezed in a few trips. They spent considerable time at the cottage, making steady improvements. But as the beach house looked better and better, and as his trees grew, Daddy declined.

One day Daddy's doctor and I were talking about his condition. "Your father is not in imminent danger," he told me, "but his time is running out. The cancer will gradually work its way into his bones, and then we can do nothing more than keep him comfortable."

My father had taken great pride in the idea that one of his boys would earn a doctorate, but I had been taking my time finishing, stretching a three-year program into five. Right then I decided the time had come for me to get off my dime and finish that degree if I wanted my father to share in the glory. In fifteen months I completed the requirements. I graduated in August, 1975, while he and Mother, surrounded by a host of family and friends, beamed at me from the audience.

In the late summer of 1976, my parents made yet another trip to the cottage, this time with Mother doing all the driving. Daddy had kept up his good humor, teasing her about her driving as he navigated them through all the country-road short cuts he loved to travel and knew so well. They had added another bathroom—a rough affair, but it served the purpose—and had installed central heating and air conditioning. They took it easy. Ate the early-bird special at Allen's Seafood Restaurant, his favorite haunt. Rode out to Phillips' Inlet, where he had spent many happy hours fishing with his sons or with various buddies who came and went. This time, though, he could only look, too tired and sick even to think of casting a line.

Mother called me, trying to control the emotion in her voice. "Bob, could you fly down here and help us get home? I don't believe I can get him home by myself. He's not in any great pain. He's just so weak."

Within a few hours, the Southern Airlines puddle jumper deposited me at the tiny Panama City airport. The next day we drove home, with Daddy seeing the cottage and its trees for the last time. After the briefest final hospital stay, the cancer that was never supposed to take his life took him away. Then, amidst tears and laughter, on a beautiful October day, with two of my brothers singing and me bringing the tribute, several hundred family members and friends gathered in my parents' church to bid Daddy farewell. Neglected prostate cancer got him.

Trees of My Own

In the spring of 1994, Linda, her mother, a teen-age niece, and I made a trip to the cottage, now ours since we had bought it from Mother in 1979. By hook and crook over several years we had managed to add vinyl siding, install new carpeting, hang miniblinds to replace the tattered curtains, retire the ancient-of-days refrigerator Daddy had found somewhere, and, at least for the fourth time, rebuild the wind-ravaged carport cover.

The front yard looked good considering the steady neglect it sustained. Nothing, however, was growing in the back yard but grotesque scrubs and wicked prickly pears. That part of the property needed some trees. On impulse, I went up to the Home Depot store and asked, "What kind of hardwood trees grow well here? I need some that thrive on neglect."

They told me what to get—ashes and elms, I believe. I went back to the house and, like my father more than twenty years earlier, planted my own generation of trees. Jennifer, our niece, and I took turns taking pictures by the trees so when they grew up, we could "remember when."

Somewhere in the midst of creating my own arboretum, it dawned on me that I was doing what my father had done. And I would look forward to the trees growing up just as my father had. Given his general good health, if the prostate cancer had not whacked him so hard, chances are he would still be around today. Though his own father had died young from heart disease brought on by heavy smoking, his mother had lived past ninety.

I could not help but think of all he had missed since his death in 1976. His good friend and fellow Baptist missionary Jimmy Carter made it to the White House. Then President Jimmy Carter invited me to join his Washington staff. Fortunately, Daddy lived to see all of his grandchildren born, but the pull of his illness kept him from enjoying the younger ones as he had the older ones. Now we have begun a crop of great-grandchildren in whom he would have taken great delight.

Much of the conflict that had bothered him greatly between the races in the South had settled down. Communism had fallen. Computers were in. Technology, with even more gadgets that would have intrigued him, surged ahead.

What's more, I believe that if he had lived, our own family would have avoided some of the turmoil that has engulfed us in these last several years. He would have provided a steadying influence that we needed, a rudder we lost at a critical time in our family's history.

As I patted the sandy soil around the trunk of the last of my trees, I thought, *Linda and I want to retire here in a few years. We've worked terribly hard, had our share of successes and knocks. I know I do not have much control over what happens to us, but I don't have to get sick from neglect.*

On our way home it hit me, maybe in a fresh way: *Daddy was about my age now when he learned about that lump.* Looking up from the magazine I was reading, I rather absent-mindedly said, "I'm going to call Dr. Regan this week and have my prostate checked. I'm not having any trouble. Never have. Had it checked about two years ago. No problem. I'm just going to get it checked again."

With hardly a break in her reading, Linda said, "Fine. Do that." Then she returned to thumbing through her magazine.

Chapter 3

The Finger Trip

"Anita, this is Bob Maddox. I want to make an appointment with Dr. Regan to have my prostate checked. It's been about two years," I said, calling the urology office at Georgetown University Medical Center in Washington, D.C.

"Let me call you back in a few minutes. Are you experiencing any difficulty?" she asked hurriedly.

"No. I just want to get it checked."

Within half an hour Anita called back to say, "Come in this morning at 11:45, if you can. He's got an opening. Besides, it won't take long."

I rushed to my office to get some work done before the appointment. Busy catching up after a week's absence in Florida, I did not look up from my desk that morning until nearly 11:30. Sammy Ray, the church's administrator and my best buddy, buzzed me. "You'd better get going for that appointment. You'll be late! And don't forget, you've got a meeting downtown as soon as you can get there after you see the doctor."

Off to the Doctor

I quickly headed for Dr. Regan's office at the huge medical complex overlooking the Potomac on the western edge of charming, historic, and bustling Georgetown. I always choose to drive from the office to Georgetown on MacArthur Boulevard, a tree-lined street through the Palisades, a cordial section of the District dating back to the turn of the century, running parallel to the river. People who have lived in the area a long time talk about the simpler days of the past when people walked to the stores, shops, movie houses, schools, and churches, or rode streetcars to Georgetown or downtown to Washington.

Since 1979, when my branch of the Maddox clan first moved to Washington for me to work in the Carter White House, we have made regular trips to the Georgetown University Medical Center. Ben, our middle son, received extensive treatment there for a chronic ear infection. Dr. James Regan and others helped Linda battle a plaguing kidney condition. Thanks to her treatment, we established a solid relationship with Dr. Regan, a gifted urologist on the Georgetown staff and a splendid human being. We also have developed a keen appreciation for the center itself. While the facility is large and bustling, we have nonetheless received excellent, reasonably personal care there, especially from the urology staff.

While I burst into the waiting room about ten minutes late for my appointment, Dr. Regan was running ten minutes later, so it worked out. Since I had not had any involvement with the hospital in more than five years, I had to fill out several forms and talk to a clerk and her computer.

Preoccupied, keeping my eyes on the clock, with fleeting

feelings that I should skip the appointment and head to my next meeting, I filled out the papers, then flipped through an outdated *Time* detailing the startling news of the death of Elvis Presley. Peeping over the magazine as people in the doctor's office do, I could see sick people coming and going, sweating from pain, gray from surgery, a few even bald from radiation. A warm feeling eased through me as I mused, *Glad I'm not sick. Just here for a checkup.*

I popped into the examining room when the nurse called my name.

"Mr. Maddox, what did you need to see Dr. Regan about today?"

"It's been about two years since I had my prostate checked, and I simply wanted Dr. Regan to make sure I'm okay."

The ubiquitous question: "Are you having any trouble?" Pen poised on the medical chart.

"No, but my father died of complications from prostate cancer, so I've always tried to keep an eye, or at least the doctor's finger, on the little rascal." I needed to laugh off some of my nervousness.

The nurse did not need the laugh. "Good idea," she said absently, continuing to write on her chart without even a mini-twinkle in her eyes. In her time, she had probably heard every lame attempt at prostate humor. "Why don't you step behind the screen. Take off your pants and shoes. Put on the gown. Dr. Regan will be in shortly."

I hate to strip in a doctor's office. It is always chilly. My sunshine-starved legs look especially white in the fluorescent glare. But I complied, of course. I hung my pants on the hook, kicked off my shoes, wrapped the one-size-fits-nobody gown around me as best I could, parked on the examining table, and waited.

I have learned that I can wait with a fair amount of forbearance if I have something to do or read. When the nurse had called me into the doctor's inner sanctum, I had dropped *Time* and grabbed an even older and more bedraggled *National Geographic*. It would keep me company until Dr. Regan exploded into the room. Doctors nearly always do that, it seems—explode, whiz, swirl into the examining room.

As I learned some fascinating information about mountain goats in Tibet, the kind of stuff you hope you remember the next time you appear on *Jeopardy,* my eyes wandered to the various posters on the wall, the genre drawn in red and blue ink showing human insides. Naturally I felt especially pulled to one detailing the male reproductive system and sporting a large circle around the area of the prostate gland. I had never paid much attention to such drawings before, but this time I studied the poster with a bit more care. For the first time, I noticed the close proximity between the prostate and the rectum. *So that's why the doctor always poked his finger where and how he did to check the prostate. Hmm!*

In a few minutes Dr. Regan burst into the tiny room. Though I had talked with him on the phone several times, I had not seen him in the flesh in about four years; fortunately, Linda had not had any serious kidney-stone attacks in some time. He looked younger than I remembered, maybe because I am getting older. Tall, handsome, and open-faced, with an aura of competence and assurance about him, he smiled readily and shook my hand.

Looking at the nurse's notes, he asked, "How old was your father when he died?"

"Sixty-seven."

"When was his cancer diagnosed?"

I told him the story of the doctor's discovery and warning, and of my father's neglect.

"Well, let's 'wave a finger' at you. Pull down your shorts. Get up on the table, lie on your left side, and pull your legs up against you. Won't take but a minute."

I knew the routine and did as he instructed.

Snap went the rubber glove. Smear went the lubricating goo. Zap went the finger. By the time I breathed again, he was through. The digital rectal examination is not really all that bad. It does not hurt, and it only takes a few minutes. It is a bit humiliating, though, to us proud males. But so is changing diapers, washing dishes, and taking out the garbage—still, we do those things anyway.

> **The exam can be a bit humiliating to us proud males.**

"Here, take the tissues. Get rid of the gel. Then put on your clothes."

In one motion I rolled off the table, pulled up my shorts, and moved behind the screen to put on my pants in preparation for dashing to my meeting. I do not know why I moved behind the screen to put on my pants. The doctor did not care, and the nurse had seen everything; I guess, by reflex, I went out of sight to zip up my fly.

Then, the medical pause.

"Mr. Maddox," Dr. Regan said, "you've got a lump on your prostate. You had your last examination about two years ago and nothing showed up?"

Stunned, I managed to stammer, "That's right."

I understood *lump*. But then the doctor began to spout a foreign language to the nurse.

"I want to do a PSA test today and schedule you for an ultrasound and a laser biopsy. Let's do that ultrasound on Friday, if you can make it. By the time you come back for the ultrasound, we'll have the results of the PSA. Any questions?"

Any questions? You have got to be kidding. Pregnant women have ultrasounds. PSA? Laser biopsy? Lumps? My head swirled. I did not come in here for this kind of non-sense. Shocked, made nearly mute by the news, more surprised than worried, I gulped and mumbled inanely, "No. See you on Friday."

"Mary, do the PSA and give Mr. Maddox instructions for the picture and biopsy."

Then the hall swallowed him up.

Shaken to my socks, but late for my appointment, I finished dressing and drove across town to my meeting. Later, I told Linda what had happened, trying to assure her by saying that Dr. Regan did not seem alarmed. We were just taking routine precautions in light of my family history.

The Biopsy

As the nurse explained to me in that first appointment, a laser biopsy is the procedure by which the doctor inserts a needle through the wall of the rectum into the lump in the prostate. The needle, sometimes called a biopsy gun, is de-signed to open once inside the prostate, take a tiny sample of tissue, then close. The needle is removed, and the sample is delivered to a laboratory that analyzes it for cancerous tissue. Technology has advanced to the point that this pro-cedure can be conducted in the doctor's office without the need for anesthesia. Biopsy of the prostate remains the most definitive test for prostate cancer to date.

Biopsies can also be taken in a cystoscopic examination, a procedure in which the doctor inserts a scope through the end of the penis, up the urethra, through the urinary tube to the bladder, and, when necessary, beyond. The fiber-optic scope allows the doctor to peer inside the bladder.

> **Biopsy remains the most defini- tive test for prostate cancer.**

While such exams are more unpleasant than laser biopsies (as I learned seeing Linda through cystoscopic examinations during her own medical difficulties), even cystoscopies have lost much of their nastiness in recent years.

Patients must make some preparations before the laser biopsy. Because the needle used must pass from the rectum (an unsanitary system) into the prostate (a clean and closed system), an enema is used about an hour before the procedure to clean out the lower track and reduce the chances of spreading an infection between the two systems.

Patients are also instructed not to take any aspirin for a period of time before the biopsy. The procedure could involve some bleeding, so it is important to avoid aspirin's blood-thinning effects.

The Role of the Prostate

This is probably as good a time as any to discuss the prostate gland itself. First, many folks mispronounce the word. It is not *prostrate*—that is the position you assumed, flat on your face, when you met Genghis Khan. The gland is pronounced *prostate,* with no second *r.*

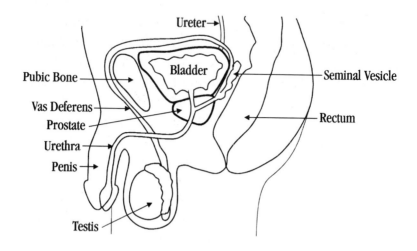

The prostate is an accessory male sex gland, actually a collection of glands enclosed in a small sack. It is responsible for producing a thick fluid that manufactures the ejaculate, the semen that transports the sperm. The testes manufacture sperm. In sexual activity, the sperm passes up through a tube, the *vas deferens,* to the prostate. The prostate and adjacent *seminal vesicles* provide the semen that carries the sperm back down through the urethra and out through the end of the penis. Shorthand: no prostate gland, no emission.

The healthy organ in a grown man is about the size of a walnut, located below the bladder and in front of the rectum. It folds around the upper part of the urethra, the tube that empties urine from the bladder. It is the prostate's position around the urethra that can cause painful, if routine, trouble for men as they get older.

Despite some popular misconceptions, the prostate is not expendable like the appendix. It plays an essential role in reproduction and in sexual performance.

Alterations in the prostate occur because of certain hormonal changes in men as they get older, but no one yet seems to know precisely why those changes take place. Studies are being conducted to find out more about the changes and how to control them, but at this writing, nothing definitive has been determined. Some of the problems may come from diet, tension, heredity, and genetic imbalance. (Recently released studies of prostate cancer point to discoveries of a genetic defect that predisposes some men to this form of cancer. This research is in its earliest stages, with a great deal more study needed to locate the specific gene responsible. If and when it is found, this particular genetic defect would probably account for only a small percentage of incidents of prostate cancer.)

African Americans and Caucasians with a family history of prostate cancer have the highest risk.

African American males, as a group, and white males with a family history of prostate maladies, have a higher rate of difficulty than the rest of the male population. Men in a culture with a low-fat diet seem to have less difficulty than those in countries where heavier foods are eaten, though there is, as yet, no proven direct link between fatty diets and prostate problems.

Not Necessarily Cancer

The prostate grows along with the human body. The problem comes for many older men when the muscle surrounding the prostate tightens or contracts, or the gland begins to grow again. Changes in the prostate can indicate cancerous or non-cancerous conditions.

Noncancerous changes are known as benign prostatic hyperplasia (BPH). An enlarged, troublesome prostate does not necessarily indicate cancer. In fact, prostate cancer typically has few warning signs in the beginning. Problems with urination, though not necessarily directly related to cancer, can be an early warning sign. But only a thorough examination can tell for sure.

Situated as the prostate is around the urethra, the second-stage changes related to BPH can restrict or squeeze shut the tube, dramatically interfering with the passage of water from the bladder. If that problem becomes severe enough, surgery may be required to reopen the tube. The technical term for that procedure is transurethral resection of the prostate (TURP). In this operation, typically done under a general anesthesia, the doctor inserts an instrument through the tip of the penis to remove the noncancerous, benign prostate tissue pressing against the urethra.

More than a few men endure restricted urination for years rather than pay the price of a few hours in the hospital and a few days at home getting better. One friend had suffered for years, allowing the doctors to give him only limited treatment. Then, while touring Europe by train, his system closed down entirely, throwing him into near-mortal agony as he went for fourteen hours unable to urinate before he could get to a doctor and a hospital to relieve the problem. Needless to say, immediately upon returning to the United States, he had surgery. Now my friend sings the praises of TURP.

Preventing Prostate Problems

Can we take care of the prostate in an effort to avoid trouble? Other than attention to diet, there is no proven therapy to ward off problems.

Dr. Sheldon Marks, in his book *Prostate and Cancer: A Family Guide* (Fisher Books, 1995), draws a close connection between diet and prostate cancer. He suggests that a prolonged diet heavy with such vegetables as broccoli, cabbage, cauliflower, Brussels sprouts, and Swiss chard, along with several servings a day of fresh fruit, "may well reduce the odds of developing cancer in the future or could even slow down a cancer you may already have."

> *All* **men should have regular checkups, especially those with a family history.**

There is anecdotal evidence of benefits from certain homeopathic regimens and extra vitamins, but no direct link between these processes and a healthy prostate gland has been established. Recently, studies have been conducted regarding certain hormone protocols that might make for a healthier prostate. At this writing, more studies need to be done before any informed medical judgment can be made.

Most cancer researchers readily agree that prostate cancer is the most frequently diagnosed tumor in American men. It is the number two cancer killer of men. (Lung cancer has the grim distinction of being number one.) With something like forty thousand deaths a year from prostate cancer, many of which could have been avoided with early detection, I say again as I have said before and will repeat often: Guys, don't sit on it! Get your prostate checked. All men should have regular checkups after they reach their fiftieth birthday—earlier, if they have any family history of prostate problems.

Chapter 4

The "C" Word

From the day of the initial examination until my next appointment, I did not labor under any particular anxieties. Friday morning I told Sammy Ray I had to go back for another test that afternoon. I hurried to get my routine work completed in case I did not feel like returning to church after the procedure.

Downing a cup of soup on the run, I went by the house for the—*shudder*—enema. That done, and with the appropriate results achieved, I waited for Linda to come from her office to drive me to the medical center. As it turned out, she could not wait with me. We arranged that she would pick me up in about an hour.

Within minutes the nurse and I were in the examining room going through a check list.

"Any aspirin?"

"No."

"You've been drinking extra liquids?"

"Yes."

"Enema?"

"Yes (groan)."

"Off with your trousers, shorts, and shoes. Dr. Regan will be right in."

"Do you have the results of the PSA?" I asked, as if I knew what PSA meant.

"Mmm, let me see." She flipped through the pages of my rapidly expanding chart. "It came back 3.4."

"What does that mean?"

"It's within tolerances, but close. If it gets beyond a 4 we get anxious."

I breathed a sigh of relief. No problem.

"By the way," I asked the nurse cautiously, "what is PSA?" Here I am living and dying by something I don't know a thing about.

"PSA means prostate specific antigen. It's a blood test that measures substances in the blood that may rise in the event of prostate cancer," she answered easily.

The Place of the PSA

Later, I learned from Dr. Regan that a Dr. Wang, a biochemist at Stanford University, discovered the prostate specific antigen, a protein. Along with others, he developed the PSA test. If the PSA protein tests high, cancer may be indicated. A high PSA count also can indicate urinary-tract or prostate infection, stones within the prostate, or a noncancerous enlargement of the gland.

The test is not entirely accurate. My problem registered within acceptable tolerances, according to the PSA test. If I had relied only on the blood test, my tumor would have gone undetected. In fact, approximately 25 percent of prostate cancers register normal on the PSA scale. Because of that possibility, the PSA should not stand alone. The American Urological Society and the American Cancer Society recommend a combination of digital rectal examination (DRE) and PSA test for Caucasian men over fifty. African American men over forty—and all men with symptoms or a history of prostate cancer in their family—should begin regular testing with some combination of digital exam and PSA measurement.

Should every man have a PSA test? The facts are not in. The medical community and the insurance industry are debating the issue. At approximately forty dollars per test, a PSA is less expensive for men than mammography is for women. And despite its shortcomings, it reveals a higher percentage of the cancers for which it was designed than do mammograms.

Yet some health-care insurance companies have begun to express misgivings about wholesale PSA testing. For instance, a major northwest health carrier has ruled it out altogether, declaring it too expensive and too inconclusive. Even fans of the PSA admit that mass-marketing campaigns fail to point out the shortcomings.

At the same time, doctors insist that if they did not offer the PSA to patients who were later diagnosed with advanced prostate cancer, they might get sued. In an article in the *Washington Post,* Andrew Wolf of the University of Virginia Health Sciences was quoted as saying, "Undiagnosed cancer is the number two or three cause of malpractice litigation."

Detecting the Danger

As Dr. Regan and I talked off and on for several months after my surgery, I learned that the digital exam also can miss a problem in the prostate. Because of the way the prostate is situated in the body, the exam allows the doctor to feel only a portion of the gland; a lump can occur in places the doctor cannot reach with his finger. In men with symptoms, the digital exam can detect 70 to 80 percent of prostate cancers. In men without symptoms, however, the exam may pick up only about one-third of all prostate cancers.

I can readily identify with this assessment. Less than two years prior to the discovery of my cancer, I had gone to another doctor, quite competent, for a physical. He performed a digital exam on me but found nothing. When I asked about the PSA test, he said he did not detect anything to warrant the test. Did he miss the lump on my prostate? Or did it not exist at that time? Did it grow enough during the intervening twenty-four months so that Dr. Regan could readily discover it? No one knows.

A good friend of mine had a different experience with prostate-cancer detection. For some months he had difficulty urinating. Because he could not fully empty his bladder, he also had to get up in the night frequently to use the bathroom. After my episode, this friend went to a urologist, who administered the PSA and performed the digital exam. Nothing out of the ordinary showed up. A year later, with the nagging symptoms persisting, he had another PSA. This time the test registered 7, well beyond the comfort zone. Back he went to the urologist, who did the digital exam again, still with no evidence of a lump. Alarmed, however, at the high PSA, the doctor zapped him with an ultrasound and biopsy, which indicated my friend did, indeed, have prostate cancer. Were the cancer and the urinary problems related? The doctor said probably not. Still, the persistence of my friend's urinary troubles kept him alert to the possibility of larger difficulties.

Another acquaintance had a history of prostate cancer in his family, so, as he grew older, he kept close watch on his own health. In his fifties he began having trouble urinating. He paid regular visits to the doctor, but nothing showed up indicating cancer. He returned regularly to the doctor because the urination problem persisted. In time, the doctors decided to do a biopsy. This procedure showed that he did have prostate cancer in its very early stages. Since he was by then in his middle sixties, the doctors gave him the choice of watchful waiting or surgery. Otherwise quite healthy, he chose the surgery, from which he has progressed steadily.

If you have any family history of prostate cancer, or any symptoms or suspicions, you have to keep pushing until all the facts are in. Remember, too, that medical science can never replace your need to assume responsibility. You surely do want to pay close attention to your body, while avoiding paranoia. Think of it like taking your car to a mechanic. You may not know exactly why it clicks and clacks like it does, but you have to take it in and tell the mechanic what to look for.

> **Medical science can never replace your need to assume responsibility.**

Timing is important. Many tumors are found too late for complete elimination, or cure. At best, about half of the prostate cancers initially diagnosed as confined to the prostate, prove, upon surgical examination, to have broken out of the gland and spread to other areas of the body.

The Trans-Rectal Ultrasound

I will never forget the events of that momentous Friday appointment. As the nurse was educating me about PSA, Dr. Regan breezed in for the Trans-Rectal Ultrasound (TRUS). In this procedure, the rectal probe bounces sound waves off the prostate gland. A computer translates those sound waves and generates a picture on a monitor screen—similar to the ultrasound a pregnant woman experiences when the doctor checks the condition of the baby she is carrying. In the Trans-Rectal procedure the picture plays the double role of informing the doctors about the condition of the prostate and guiding them as they take a biopsy or consider other treatments.

"We're going to make an ultrasound of your prostate," Dr. Regan said first. "You can see what we're doing on the screen there at your head. I'll take a look, make the pictures; then we'll do the biopsy. The biopsy gun will take ten snips. You'll feel something like a mild bee sting when we take our core samples. This only takes a few minutes. Okay? Any questions? Let's go, then."

I resisted the temptation to tell him I did not give a rip about seeing my prostate on the screen. I just wanted everything to be all right, and I wanted to get on with my life. Then I felt the probe in my rectum.

"There, on the screen, is your prostate," exclaimed the doctor, sounding for all the world like a boy who has just made his first Erector-set bridge go up and down. All I could think of was that ninety thousand dollar thing, poking around areas of my body I had never even thought about.

"And there is the lump," he proudly announced. "Now we'll begin the biopsy."

Almost instantly I felt the "bee sting." Dr. Regan's instrument seemed to inhale, pull, and snip. Then he moved his snipper and repeated the procedure. Sweat popped out on my face. I had certainly felt far worse pain in my life, though pain is not my favorite thing. But this one kept hitting me way up inside my body, filling me with sensations that made me want to pounce off the table. I hardly breathed.

"Four more snips and we're done," he said.

I began to count, fighting a dark dizziness.

One!

Two, oh my!

Three—almost there.

And four! Done. Blessed exit. Tissues. Get dressed.

Thus ended my first and, I pray, last experience with a Trans-Rectal Ultrasound. On a ten-point pain scale, the procedure probably registered only a three, but I would not want to encounter TRUS on a regular basis.

Face to Face with My Mortality

With my clothes back on I turned to the doctor. "Okay, Dr. Regan, tell me what you think. I was so stunned the other day when you found the lump that I did not ask you any questions."

"Mr. Maddox, I'm as sure as I can be that it's cancer," he said with a strong note of understanding and dread in his voice.

Cancer. That's what he said: Cancer. The big, bad word. I had stood with other family members and friends across the years as they got the big "C" laid on them. But this was me. Cancer applied to Numero Uno really takes some getting used to. An alien had invaded. Some sort of body snatcher stalked me. I am not quite as clean inside as I used to be.

As never before, I was forced to face my own mortality. I could die from this; my father had. The news media regularly reported yet another death from prostate cancer. What was to prevent me from walking down that same one-way path? Though not terribly afraid of death, I certainly did not want it now. My wife and children, my grandsons needed me. And I needed them. It is easy to gloss over death. But if you think about it, especially imagining that it is your name on the tombstone, the word *death* does not have a great deal of lilt to it.

In the course of my life, I had lost (or maybe I should say *surrendered*) much of my fear of death. It was not that I had shaken my fist in the face of bony death and told him to take a hike. I attribute my resolve to the presence of God that came to me as a teen-ager, removing fear of death as a stalking predator to my thinking.

I remember the moment vividly. I had just turned sixteen. As I was lying in bed one night, my mind turned to my own death. Almost in the same moment, a strong but sweet—yes, sweet—Presence moved upon me, bringing the assurance that death need hold no terror for me—nor, for that matter, for any person of faith.

> **I do not fear what lies beyond death.**

To be sure, I have not invited death. The idea of a terrible or lingering death makes me recoil. But I do not fear what lies beyond death. I value the biblical witness that portrays the death of the faithful as part of the plan and grace of God. Contemporary studies on death and dying point to an experience of brightness and well-being in which I find comfort. I feel fully persuaded that, ultimately, we have nothing to fear from death.

Based on my having come to terms with death, the prospect of the eventual operation did not terrorize me. When my hour arrived, I went through the swinging doors of the surgical suite dreading terribly what lay ahead of me, but I did not fear death. I was not being stoic. My lack of fear grew from faith in God that had come to me as an expression of grace. I went secure in the knowledge that I was all right no matter what happened on the operating table.

As a minister I have stood by the bed of people as their life ebbed away. I have walked with uncounted families as they dealt with the death of a loved one. Through it all, I have come to the steady conviction that as I have lived in the Lord, so will I die in the Lord. To be sure, I am not eager for my life to come to a close—I have too much living I want to do, as well as a good deal of patching up that I must do. And the prospect of a long and drawn-out death holds no charm. But the final end will be all right. Wherever God is, I will be there also, thanks to his grace.

Telling the News

Dr. Regan did not let the conversation end with cancer. "The good news is that by coming in early as you did, before you had any trouble, I'm just as convinced that it is completely contained in the prostate. To make sure, I want to schedule you for a complete bone scan and a CAT scan. We'll do those right away. As soon as the lab has had a look at these samples, we'll talk some more and chart out a course of action."

Then he looked at me intently. "I know this is a shocker. But you will be all right. You'll have some adjustments. But when it's over, you'll be just fine." Then he added, "You may have some side effects from the biopsy—bleeding, etc. Lydia will explain all that to you. If you have any problems, call me at home."

With that word of assurance, he wrote his home phone number on the back of his card. "We'll talk on Tuesday or Wednesday, just as soon as the lab report comes back."

Linda still had not come back from her appointment to pick me up. Rather than wait in Dr. Regan's crowded sitting room, I found another lounge area, all but empty and somewhat darkened. It was near the elevator, where I could spot Linda when she arrived, yet be away from the constant flow of human traffic.

Cancer?

Me?

Surgery?

My mind reeled. What sort of complications? What "adjustments"? What were the short-term and long-term implications? And what about my church? The last pastor had died of cancer after a lingering illness. Would they be mad at me for putting them through this again? What sort of expense is involved?

> **Illness never comes at a convenient time.**

And what about Linda?! Illness never comes at a convenient time. But this one was roaring down on us like a freight train. Less than a year before, her father had died after a two-year bout with a debilitating disease. During much of that time, especially the last twelve months of his life, Linda had kept the roads and the airways between Washington and Georgia hot with her traveling to help her mother manage his illness and deal with some terribly complicated extended-family problems. Now this.

The elevator door opened and out she bounded, looking anxiously for me.

"Hi," I said from my semidark corner.

"Are you through? I couldn't get back any sooner. The traffic was awful. Are you all right? How do you feel? Did it hurt much?"

"Yep, I'm done. Let's go. I feel sort of spooky. I'll tell you about it when we get outside," I said, heading for the elevator.

With just the two of us standing there waiting for the elevator to come, she looked at me and asked, "Is it cancer?"

That was the first moment in the several days since this minidrama had begun to unfold that either one of us had asked that question. It had all happened so quickly. From the appointment on Tuesday to this biopsy on Friday, we had not had much space to talk about anything.

"Yes. He's as sure as he can be that it is."

With that, the elevator opened, and we stepped into a car full of people.

Linda says she died a thousand times on that ride from Dr. Regan's fourth-floor office.

Walking into the brilliant four o'clock Washington afternoon, I rapidly began to tell her what had happened, starting with the end of the story first—that Dr. Regan had every confidence we could manage the problem with no long-lasting effects.

"It's contained, and surgery will correct the problem," I assured her, quoting the doctor.

Linda drove us home through the rush-hour traffic, easing out of the Georgetown Hospital complex, heading away from the city on Reservoir Road, then to Foxhall and Canal and across the picturesque Key Bridge spanning the Potomac River between Washington and Virginia. For a change, we hardly noticed the traffic, so intently were we talking about what had happened.

By the time we had made the twenty-minute drive to our home in North Arlington, I felt completely washed out. I had no pain. So far, none of the possible side effects of the procedure had appeared, but I could hardly bring myself to put one foot in front of the other. Linda planted me on the couch, than dashed to her office for yet one more appointment.

The What and Why of Cancer

Before we leave this chapter, let's answer again the persistent question *What is cancer?*

Dr. Regan described cancer to me as a condition in which normal cell growth goes wild. Cells are constantly coming and going, generating, dying. Cancer throws this normal recycling process off, creating hyperactivity. Cancer in the prostate gland usually manifests as a tumor that grows and grows. As long as the tumor is contained within the gland itself, surgery offers great odds for cure. Unchecked, the cancer can break out of the prostate, spreading to nearby lymph nodes and other organs, including the bone marrow. Testosterone, an essential male hormone under normal conditions, manufactured in the testicles and injected directly into the blood stream, actually fuels prostate cancer. As long as the body produces testosterone, prostate cancer can grow and spread.

Medical science has come up with stunning under-standings in recent years that point us toward a definitive answer to the *what* of cancer. But full answers have not come yet explaining the *why.* Thanks, however, to concerted efforts on the part of thousands of dedicated professionals, cancer patients stand a much better chance of surviving to-day, even though a maddening array of questions remains unanswered.

Chapter 5

Getting Ready

It is part of my nature to believe that you do what you have to do. It is a trait picked up from my parents. They were both born a few years into the twentieth century and came from solid yet modest families themselves. They had children, moved, changed jobs, or took on this or that project with hardly a backward glance. They just marched on—rarely, if ever, pondering the past. They were masters at rolling with the punches. For instance, I never heard my father lament his cancer. He lived for today: Do everything you can for now, then head on out.

I inherited a good measure of that plow-ahead mentality. I also have earned a few medals as a champion procrastinator, especially when I bump into a situation I cannot readily figure out. I grieve over some of the messes I have made along the way because I put off till next year what I should have done today.

After hearing Dr. Regan's preliminary diagnosis, I realized instinctively I had come to an important turn in the road. As never before, I faced my own suffering and death. Indeed, my entire family faced some new ingredients in their lives because of the doctor's findings. I believed that, with my family's support, I could manage the curve, but I did not know how well I would do.

Perhaps as a way to deal with the larger picture—and unable to do anything personally about my prostate—I began preparing for the disruption that lay ahead for my family and me.

After much discussion with the doctor and my family, we projected the date of the surgery, if it had to be done, about five weeks hence. Fortunately, prostate cancer usually grows slowly; next-day surgery is rarely necessary. That time differential would give us space to get ready for the ordeal. What's to get ready? Such items as a will, a living will, funeral arrangements in case they should be necessary, and medical-insurance details.

Having seen families left in chaos with a sudden death, I determined to set my affairs in order before surgery.

Preparing for the Worst

Since we have very few holdings, I did not believe my will needed much attention. I made sure Linda knew I had it tucked away on the top shelf of my bedroom closet.

Next, the living will. Like many aging Americans, I have a profound horror of becoming a burden to my family in the case of a lingering illness. I typed out a brief statement that I faxed to the doctor's office along with some insurance information they needed.

Later, Dr. Regan jokingly said, "Man, you didn't waste any time with that living will! I don't believe anything catastrophic will happen, but you've certainly let us know what you want." I simply informed the medical staff that I refused any sort of heroic efforts to keep me alive if something went sour during surgery. I rejected extraordinary life-support systems.

In the course of research for this book, I came across some disturbing articles speaking to the problem of living wills and the avoidance of extraordinary care simply to forestall death. For instance, according to an exhaustive study recently completed under a grant from the Robert Wood Johnson Foundation, patients' expressed desire to avoid dramatic medical treatment is consistently ignored by their families and physicians. Either physicians do not know of the patients' instructions, or they choose to ignore them.

One doctor at Georgetown University Hospital who was especially helpful with this book said that doctors are in the business of saving lives and that when to apply life-support systems and when to withdraw them are two of the most difficult decisions a doctor faces. He explained that sometimes a patient appears to be doing well when suddenly a medical crisis hits, and the staff is obligated to exert as much care as possible to see the person through the problem. In some events, the crisis does not go away and the patient remains on life-support technology. "What do we do then?" the doctor asked. Does the doctor's judgment override a living will? "Sometimes it does," he said, "though I would certainly do all I could to honor the patient's expressed wishes."

Families, who fully understand their loved ones' desires to avoid involved treatment, frequently fall into disagreement when a medical crisis occurs. They cannot agree on how to apply the principles laid down earlier in the living will.

With my will and living will taken care of, I turned my attention to funeral arrangements. As a minister for many years, I have seen families suddenly experience the death of one of their own with no clue about what to do next. Several years before my prostate troubles, preparing for a long business trip to India, I had written out funeral instructions to spare my family added stress in the event of my death. Without going into that particular envelope, I knew my plans had not changed, so I did not have to fret long over those details.

I checked my life insurance to make sure the policies were in good order and located where Linda could get them if necessary.

Next, I checked on my medical insurance. I called our major carrier to let them know of the impending surgery so they could provide any necessary preadmittance clearance. The policy was a good one, yet it had a fairly high deductible and a heavy co-payment plan.

A couple of years earlier I had received an ad from one of our gasoline-credit-card companies about a new cancer policy. For a modest monthly premium I could insure Linda and me with supplemental coverage. With no thought that I would ever need it, I nevertheless took out the policy. A time or two I had almost let it drop, but in the end I had not done so. Now I called to make sure the policy was in order.

"You're in good standing," the customer service representative assured me. Between the two carriers, I calculated most of my expenses would be covered. (I learned later that I was wrong. Read your cancer policy very carefully!)

Spreading the News

Of course, I did not talk about the cancer outside the family until I had heard from Dr. Regan. But as soon as I had the final word that all tests had come back positive, we decided to let people know.

Our children received a full briefing on the situation and what to expect. I called my mother and my three brothers. We told Linda's family.

As pastor of a church, I felt a responsibility to avoid playing any kind of games with the people I served. I told the church's elected officers, asking for their prayers and support. Then, I wrote a succinct letter to the entire congregation, relating to them what the doctor had said about successful surgery and a reasonably quick recovery.

We let friends in other parts of the country know—not so much by direct calling as by indirect word of mouth. If we happened to be talking on the phone, I naturally told them what I faced and asked them to pass the word along.

Soon, however, I grew weary of talking about it all. I wanted a recording: "Hello, you have reached Bob Maddox. Let me tell you about my forthcoming operation."

Searching for Significance

Other matters did loom that would prove quite vexing. As a reasonably reflective human being—complete with a doctorate in theology—I thought a great deal about the *meaning* of the illness.

Following a schedule set many months previously, the last sermon I preached before the surgery had to do with a search for meaning. That is nothing so unusual for a minister to talk about. But this one had special significance as I cast around for the meaning of this new episode in my life and the life of my family. Would the illness become a framework within which I could work on important areas of concern? While I do not believe God visits illness on us, sometimes, in the course of dealing with illness, we can realign some fundamental dimensions of our lives. For me, the meaning of the illness is wrapped up in the necessity and opportunity to find new depth in my relationships with my wife and family and to focus more clearly on what really matters.

I did not need a wake-up call from my prostate to know that frantic living for the past several years had made for many loose ends emotionally, financially, professionally, and spiritually. The crisis of the operation grabbed my attention, pushing me to get serious about these areas of greatest concern.

For instance, unremitting stress, much of it self-inflicted, had taken its toll on my emotions, pushing feelings and easy communication further and further inside of me. To a significant degree, I had chosen to fortify myself from serious emotional involvement, even with members of my family. At first, when life became es-

The meaning of my illness was wrapped up in the need to find new depth in my relationships and to focus more clearly on what really matters.

pecially tedious, I told myself I could still carry on in my little fort, that no one would notice the quiet distances I had created. Soon, however, Linda and the children began to question me. I explained that the pressures of life had gotten to me but that I was fine. They did not buy my answers. They began to insist I tear down the fort, come outside myself and engage in serious living again. I agreed. Still, though, I have not pulled down all the walls I had built up. In some ways I do not want to pull them down. I have become rather comfortable behind them. At the same time, I am acutely aware that such barriers really do interfere with the free flow of important relationships.

A Painful Prognosis

My emotional life took a real beating the afternoon Dr. Regan called to confirm officially the diagnosis of cancer.

"I want to schedule the further tests we talked about, the bone scan and the CAT scan," he said. "I do not think they will show anything new because I do not believe it has spread anywhere. But we'll want to make sure."

"What do you think you will have to do?" I asked, palms moist, heart beating faster, eyes somewhat glazed over with anxiety.

"I'd like to sit down with you and Linda after we know precisely what we're looking at. For now, I can say I believe we will have to remove the entire prostate gland, perform a radical prostatectomy. That's the only sure way to get the cancer. It also provides the best insurance against future problems."

Then, in my best clinical voice, I asked, "What are the implications of a complete removal?"

"Well," he said thoughtfully, "you will have the possibility of some incontinence, though I do not expect that it will be prolonged. And you could experience some difficulty achieving an erection." I was already dizzy, but he continued. "We've got some new techniques we can use if either of those conditions is a problem. I do not want to minimize the side effects, but I hasten to say that each patient is different. We'll walk with you and Linda every step of the way."

> **A man's persona is so wrapped up in his sexuality.**

The mention of impotence struck home. A man's persona is so wrapped up in his sexual ability that the doctor's words ran through me like a cold wind. Across the years, Linda and I had enjoyed a happy sex life. Recently, however, as with so many couples, the pressures of life had taken their toll on our relationship. I kept telling myself, "We've got time. Not to worry! We'll work and love it through." Now, to my great dismay, I realized we had rounded a new corner that could substantively change our life together. Time was an irreplaceable commodity. I felt great sadness at the doctor's words. Grief, anger at myself, and a profound sense of loss threatened to overwhelm me.

I decided not to tell Linda all the doctor had said—crazy, I know. But I believed that if she did not know the full extent of the operation I could avoid dealing with part of it myself. Silly. But that is an old, old pattern that is tough for me to break. Under the guise of protecting others from bad news, I was actually only protecting myself—and not doing that very well. Finally, no one got protected. (In fact, no one really needed protecting.)

Of course, Linda, smart and perceptive as she is, quickly figured things out. We made some good efforts at dealing with the emotional problems we faced. I regretted that we did not get far enough along during the weeks of preparation. Still, I hoped we laid the groundwork for an invigorated relationship based on what happened down the line as my body and spirit reknit.

No Good Time

The operation hit us at a time of financial stress. For sixteen years we had had one or more of our children in college or graduate school. In 1986, Linda had begun her own carpet and interiors business, an enterprise that did well for several years, despite a lack of capital. However, a series of setbacks, unfortunate decisions, a local recession, and generally frantic living had exacted a high toll on the business. Those many weeks Linda spent in Georgia during her father's lingering illness and subsequent death had been the *coup de grâce*.

Exacerbating the financial stress was my decision to re-enter the pastorate. Just prior to the onset of Linda's dad's illness, I had left my position as executive director of a national religious-liberty organization to accept the pastorate of Briggs Memorial Baptist Church, taking a stiff salary reduction in the process. It was a move that I wanted to make, that I felt spiritually compelled to take. But with Linda's income reduced, too, we had really begun to sweat.

Ben, our splendid second son, who had worked with Linda in the business for five years, took a job with a local architect, a move we encouraged and blessed. That shift led to

59

our decision to close her business and salvage what we could. Many people in the carpet and interiors business had come to know and respect Linda's ability and integrity, so several offers came when she made it known she was going to make a change. After careful consideration, in early 1994, she merged her business with another company, a smart and ultimately profitable move, but one that amounted to starting over again. She was working incredibly hard to build up the new business, handle some of the fallout from her own company, help me at the church, and still look for ways to have a semblance of a life. And now this!

Professionally, the operation found me in better shape, though not on the mark as I had intended. I had accepted the pastorate in order to focus on pastoral ministry and writing. Now, the church, though still struggling to come out of several years of severe decline, was showing definite signs of vitality. Thanks to the combined efforts and prayers of veteran members, fortified by a wonderful new group of young adults, we were making a significant difference in the life of the church.

But I had not made much progress as a writer. Many forces had come along to pull me away from what I believe to be a key focus of my life. In short, the stuff of life had cluttered my days, interfering with the second love of my professional life: writing. I recalled the words from the Old Testament: "Why spend money on what is not bread, and your labor on what does not satisfy?" (Isa. 55:2).

Taking Spiritual Inventory

With the surgery a few weeks away, the most important aspects of my life came to the front of my brain, especially internal conversations about my faith. Driving back and forth from home to work, sitting in numbing denominational meetings, idly watching television, walking around the block to build up stamina for the surgery, my mind floated to my faith. Not my public, in-the-pulpit religion, but the basic, operational, generative relationship to God that animated me as a person.

During those weeks, I took a spiritual inventory for the first time in a long time. For some people, their jobs, sports, investments—you name it—frame their lives. Faith provides my window on life. Faith has been my primary point of reference. Am I some sort of goody two shoes? Hardly. Despite my strong beliefs, I have still managed to fall into some pretty deep holes. Nonetheless, the impending operation forced me to look hard at my life, checking out my relationship with God in ways I had not felt it necessary to do in a while.

> **I took a spiritual inventory for the first time in a long time.**

From about age sixteen, the Christian perspective has framed my macro and micro outlook on life, particularly my deep belief that the quantum-physics, big-bang God has moved in human history uniquely on our behalf. I see God's movement through many great spiritual leaders past and present, most uniquely in his Son, Jesus of Nazareth.

Growing up in an Atlanta, Georgia, Baptist family in the forties and fifties exposed me to a fair share of traditional religion. On the rarest of occasions, as a teen-ager, I encountered Sunday school teachers and youth leaders who could touch something fairly deep within my spirit. These men and women stand out as important shapers of my beliefs and outlooks. Our well-meaning pastors rarely inspired me, though I knew they cared about our family. I heard my share of hellfire, no-drinking, no-smoking, no-dancing, no-going-to-movies preaching, some of which still has a hold on me. With all their failings, however, these Baptist churches and the activities they generated provided a gathering place for our family and closest friends. In those early-television, very-few-automobile years, we young people went to church Sunday morning, Sunday evening, and Wednesday evening, too, enduring the services so we could get on with the important stuff. Church socials, get-togethers at one another's houses, and, later, when some of us began to drive, going to Hensler's Barbecue or to the Varsity were the real stuff of life. Of course, the major part of our church-oriented religious life had nothing to do with biblical religion, but we had a good time and managed to stay out of most serious trouble.

Looking back on those teenage years, I realize that the uncomplicated frolic we enjoyed after formal services conveyed an important, if unconscious, point about church as a trustworthy, fun community—not a bad lesson to learn. Because of those happy experiences, I came into adulthood and vocational ministry with positive attitudes toward the church. I have managed to lead the congregations in which I have worked toward that more upbeat, affirming mode rather than the "cast 'em into hell" profile of some groups.

Rather than feeling restricted or bound by faith, I have found it wonderfully liberating. Likewise, while taking the Bible's teachings with the utmost seriousness, I have found breathtaking freedom through the sweep of biblical revelation to figure out for myself the whos, whys, and wherefores of life. Of course, I have no neat answers to life's deepest complexities. I have frequently lost my moorings. More often than not, I have failed to live up to my own best understandings. Still, a basic faith in God has served as the touchstone and the framework of my life.

> **Rather than feeling restricted by faith, I have found it wonderfully liberating.**

Benchmarks for Living

Facing a serious operation, I realized I needed to get to the bottom line of what makes my life tick. Lots of living, hurting, crying, hoping, helping, and working have helped boil down my own operational faith to two key benchmarks that have stood me in good stead.

The Grace of God

The grace of God—that is, his willingness to stay with me, put up with my nonsense, love me in spite of my lack of love—is the linchpin of my operational faith, pulling all other aspects of my life together.

I have discovered that even folks who know nothing about the Bible or about Christianity know the old hymn "Amazing Grace." I vividly recall a highly charged political gathering winding down around a swimming pool. Some of the pols were about three sheets to the wind from too much booze, and they broke out in round after round of that very hymn. Maybe political hacks feel a special need for a good measure of God's grace after a hard day making hash of the opponent!

But what is grace? Probably you have your own working definition. It is the way your spouse treats you despite the fact that you acted silly at the office Christmas party. It is the way your children give you a hug on your fiftieth birthday even though you and they know you muffed it a lot as a parent.

I translate this compelling experience of grace to mean that God is on my side, pulling for me—with cancer or clean as a whistle. This is not cheap. Grace is not the buss on the cheek from a wimpish, soft, heavenly Sugar Daddy. The grace of God does not set aside the consequences of our dumb mistakes, sin, and evil. It does flow in generosity from the nature of God as a resonating *yes* to all who will accept it. Neither is grace a pie-in-the-sky in-the-sweet-by-and-by sentiment. It is a daily operating principle.

Grace told me that God would see me through the operation, regardless of the outcome. Grace does not provide an abundance of neat formulations about the human condition, but it does say that the One who sees the *before* and the *after* has become part of our *now*. Grace works.

A User-Friendly Divine Providence

Along with grace, I rely heavily on a concept I call the user-friendly providence of God. Paul, the most prolific of biblical writers and no stranger to upsets and dislocations, encapsulated this principle for me in a verse from his letter to the Romans: "All things work together for good as we make a commitment to move in concert with the will of God" (Rom. 8:28, my translation).

Believe me, in some of my more ragged moments I have clung to that message from God as a shipwrecked sailor clings to the flotsam. I could see no immediate good coming from my prostate cancer. Still, I trusted God to help me see the positive for myself and then, if and when possible, to pass it on to others.

Many loose ends remain. My sins and failings rise up before me. But in God's eyes, a big *OK* is written by my name.

An Eternal Perspective

These basics constantly provide a wellspring of hope and a sense of future. Novocain for life's hurts? Maybe, to some degree. But what is wrong with Novocain when the dentist starts to pull a tooth? More than a quick fix, however, these benchmarks provide a perspective, a window on the world in which I live.

For many years, as a student of human nature, I have found that it takes a great deal of effort to make systemic changes in our lives. Like a huge mountain that has stood for eons, our personality patterns get set. Frequently, neither serious reverses, nor illness, nor even tragedy can effect change.

With that in mind, only time will tell what will come of this episode in my life. Nothing of consequence will occur if I do not make it happen; it remains to be seen what kind of realignments will actually take place. Still, those episodes of reflection helped me gain a better hold on my life and provided a reasonably firm place to stand as the day for the operation drew ever closer.

Chapter 6

The Pre-Op Minuet

Dr. Regan and I had our big talk late one afternoon during the second week of April when he gave me the news of cancer in the prostate. As I pressed him for more answers, he interjected, "Mr. Maddox, understandably you have many questions. I am sure Linda does also. Let's get these other tests done; then the three of us can sit down together and go through the whole thing. Call my office in the morning to arrange a bone scan, a CAT scan, and appointments with the Georgetown blood bank. I want you to give at least three units of your own blood so that we can transfuse it back into you if the need arises. With nearly five weeks before the surgery, you will have time to make the donations. Okay?" And then the favorite benediction of doctors, "Call me if you have any questions. You've got my home phone. Don't hesitate."

Before Dr. Regan hung up, I stammered, "I know about giving blood, but what's a bone scan? What's a CAT scan?"

"Mr. Maddox," he said gently, "I'm as sure as I can be that your cancer is contained in the prostate. I want to make sure, however. These two procedures will confirm my hopes.

The bone scan gives us an image of your skeletal structure. The CAT scan does essentially the same thing for your major organs. Okay? See you soon." Later, he pointed out that not all doctors ask for these procedures, especially so early in the process. However, he felt he needed them to make sure the cancer had not spread.

My doctor had no way of knowing that neither of my insurance plans would pay for these tests. Since I was hardly ever sick, I had not met the high deductible requirement with my primary carrier. My gasoline-company-credit-card carrier, I learned to my dismay, did not pay anything toward tests of any kind; they only covered direct treatment of cancer. As a result, I got hung with a bill for twelve hundred dollars for procedures that even Dr. Regan said were not absolutely essential for my treatment. Despite all my screaming and yelling, I had to pay up. (How can you avoid such situations? Ask questions. Make sure you know what your carriers will and will not pay.)

Other fellow prostate-cancer-surgery friends who went to different doctors and hospitals report slightly different pre-op procedures, variations on my themes. Almost all gave blood ahead of time. Some had bone and CAT scans. Others underwent a different set of tests. Bottom line: doctors have differing philosophies and approaches.

Take responsibility for your treatment. Leave nothing to chance. Ask questions and make suggestions. You are not out to please the doctor but to get well. Your life and mental health are on the line. Take care of yourself. If an extra test or two help your own peace of mind, talk with the doctor.

One friend had serious questions about the treatment he was receiving but, since he had developed a friendship with the physician over several years, hesitated to press his concerns. Instead, he moaned to his son about the doctor's lack of attention. Finally, the son said, "Dad, talk with your doctor. Make him tell you what he's doing. He's human like the rest of us."

"What if I hurt his feelings? What if he gets upset with me?"

"Look, if you're worried about his feelings, send him some flowers. But either get your answers or change doctors."

My friend asked the questions, then changed doctors. I never heard if he sent flowers.

Hearing Voices

First thing next morning after our conversation, I called Dr. Regan's office. "Lydia, this is Bob Maddox. That May 25 date for the surgery you and I talked about suits the doctor, according to a conversation I had with him yesterday afternoon. He wants me to have a bone scan and a CAT scan, as well as to give three units of my own blood. What do we do?"

"I'll call you back."

Within an hour or so, Lydia called me back.

"The Nuclear Medicine Department can do the bone scan next Monday morning at eight thirty. Can you be there? Then the radiology lab can do the CAT scan on Wednesday morning. You'll need to call both labs and get specific instructions. I will also fax you what details I have. Neither is complicated. Neither hurts. Here's the number for the blood bank. Call and make your own appointments for autologous donations."

Nuclear medicine! Was I going to get nuked? All I wanted

was a simple prostate operation. I certainly did not want to get tied up with nuclear stuff. Do you come out of the lab glowing? And what in the world is *autologous donation?* Nonetheless, I called the blood bank and made three appointments, one each for the next three weeks.

The Nuclear Medicine Voice said, "Be here before eight thirty. You don't have to fast prior to coming in. We'll give you a radioactive injection." (They *were* going to nuke me!) "We'll wait a couple of hours for the medicine to travel through your body; then we'll do the bone scan."

The CAT scan would be a bit more complicated. "Mr. Maddox," the CAT Scan Voice said, "you'll need to fast before you come in. Do not eat or drink anything after midnight. Come to the lab by 8:45 A.M. and we'll get you started." You know, I've always wondered what people eat or drink after midnight, especially at my age. I'm fast asleep well before that hour arrives.

In case you or someone close to you has to undergo these procedures, let me tell you of my experience as a way to increase your understanding and perhaps lessen the trauma. Your reaction will, of course, be different from mine.

The Bone Scan

Just before eight thirty on Monday morning I made my appearance for the bone scan at the Nuclear Medicine Department, tucked away in the upper reaches of the vast Georgetown Hospital complex. A sign directed me to the lab's waiting room, a room like any other medical waiting room, at least when it comes to furniture and old magazines. What was different was the drama of the people—the nuke waiting room throbbed quietly with suffering and anxiety.

Needless to say, not much happy chatter floated back and forth between the patients. In fact, an eery quiet gripped the room.

Across from me sat a bright young teen-age boy, the picture of health. Maybe his coach had sent him for some kind of checkup so he could play soccer or baseball. Then I saw and felt his anxious parents. My second glance at the boy revealed the look of quiet terror in his own eyes and I knew, in a hurry, that he faced more than a pregame physical.

To my left sat a lightly tanned man I judged to be about forty-five. He wore a neat jogging outfit and new tennis shoes of some distinctive style. His sandy, wavy hair curled back over his high, handsome, bronzed forehead. With every ounce of energy in his body, he had determined to remain twenty and had made a good go at it. I had to wonder, however, at the force that had invaded his twenty-something, forty-five-year-old body that could quickly mitigate all his fountain-of-youth ministrations.

To be sure, though our little cell of human suffering remained still and quiet, the great engines of the mighty healing machine around us pulsed, chugged, hurried, and hassled right outside the door.

The receptionist never stopped punching stuff into her computer. Technicians came and went chatting about children, ball games, this or that problem within their department. Were they indifferent to our needs? I don't think so, but it was easy to feel that we were just commercial entities in the maw of a huge industry that made its living off pain, fear, and death.

After about twenty minutes, a young man poked his head into the waiting room and called my name. He led me into a surprisingly grungy lab room and parked me on a stool.

The griminess and general disarray surprised me. Dr. Regan's offices, by contrast, were fresh, orderly, and clean. This was a pit.

The technician reached into a cabinet with the familiar radioactive emblem on its door and prepared to nuke me.

"Mr. Maddox," he recited in medical monotone for the umpteenth time, "this will hardly hurt. I will inject you with a very small radioactive dose. It will move through your body for the next couple of hours. Please return by eleven o'clock this morning for the bone scan. You can do what you choose in the meantime. You should feel no aftereffects from the injection. If you have any problems or suffer any side effects, please return quickly to this lab."

With easy skill, he popped me with the stuff. Sure enough,

> **It's easy to feel like a commercial entity in the maw of a huge industry called HEALTH CARE.**

his stick did not hurt. Though I waited for nuclear-explosion warning bells to go off in my head, nothing happened. I left his lab and returned to my nearby office for the next two hours. I have to admit I felt like a Chernobyl accident waiting to happen. Fortunately, I suffered no sudden bumps or abrasions that might have detonated me. Having no side effects, I showed up at the appointed hour at the nuclear medicine warren.

This time, I hardly had time to sit down with one of the

bedraggled magazines before a young Indian woman called my name. She shook my hand and, in her delightful British-Indian accent, pointed me to a room at the end of the hall. I followed her.

"This," she explained, "is the bone-scan machine. You can keep on all your clothes except your shoes." What a relief. "Climb up on the table and lie still. The machine moves down your body making a full picture of your skeletal structure. The injection has moved through your body making it possible for the scan to photograph your bones and capture anything out of the ordinary. It takes about twenty minutes for the camera to move the length of your frame. I will strap your feet together so we can have a straight shot of your legs."

With that, she pulled my feet together and wrapped a piece of elastic around them so they would remain upright. She pushed and shoved me around on the flat, hard table, placed a pillow under my head, then pulled the camera down within inches of my nose.

"Lie still and we will begin. If you have any difficulty, let me know."

I could hear her in another part of the room throwing switches. Then, silently, relentlessly, the big camera began to move down my body. I took a nap. No need to waste twenty minutes in the middle of the day. If I could not read or snack, I could doze, and that is what I did. Frankly, I remember almost nothing of the bone scan. No, she did not have to wake me up. When the machine stopped, I awoke but lay still until the technician told me I could move.

"Please, Mr. Maddox, if you will be so kind as to wait in the patient lounge until I have developed the pictures."

Minutes later she stuck her head into the waiting room

and motioned for me to follow her. Somewhat shaken she said, "We have a problem. You have a large spot on your lung. We must make another picture."

Immediately my blood pressure shot out the roof. A large spot on my lung! Wait just a minute. A spot on my prostate, yes. But a spot on my lung? No way! What in the world is going on?

Then she showed me a miniature picture of my skeleton, spooky in itself. Sure enough, right there on my left chest screamed a large spot.

"Before you become too alarmed," she said, "it could be a spot of contamination on your shirt. Would you please remove your shirt and let me examine it."

I fairly tore the shirt off my back and thrust it at her. She examined it carefully, holding it up to the light, taking it into the lab.

"No," she said in a minute. "Your shirt is clean."

So was my underwear, but maybe not for long. What about that spot?

"I want to make another picture on a different machine, without your shirt." With that, she had me sit on a stool and lean up against another large x-ray gadget.

"Hold your breath when I tell you to. Then exhale slowly."

I obeyed unquestioningly and then, once again, found myself back in the lounge.

"We found the problem," she told me in a few minutes. "The pillow on which you lay had a spot of nuclear contaminant. The new picture is perfectly clear." And she showed me the newest picture of my chest, this one free of the spot.

"How in the world did some of the nuclear stuff get on the pillow?" I asked.

She shrugged, thanked me for my patience, and told me I was free to go.

Just another day in the inner sanctum of a house of modern medicine.

The CAT Scan

Wednesday morning I reported for the CAT scan—computerized axial tomography, to be exact. This procedure calls for "patient participation." The Phone Voice had told me to fast after midnight. Upon my arrival, someone did a quick workup on me: blood pressure, temperature, and a list of "have you ever . . . ?" questions.

"Now, please go into the little room and take all your clothes off. Put on the gowns you will find lying on the bench."

I knew I could not keep my clothes on too long. I ducked into the tiny room, undressed, and pulled on two hospital gowns, one for the front and one for the rear. Later in the operation process, after all sense of modesty had long gone, it occurred to me that I could probably have just stripped off raw, paraded from the dressing room to the lab, and no one would have noticed. But at that stage I still clung to some commitment to covering my nudity in public. The worst lay ahead of me, however. The technician approached me with a large pitcher of white stuff.

"Before we can do the scan, you've got to drink all this liquid. It's really not too bad. Just wolf it down as rapidly as you can. This is our mint-flavored variety," she said enthusiastically. "Think of it as a Baskin-Robbins milk shake."

Sure, lady.

"What is it?" I inquired, my morning coffeeless stomach already quivering.

"Barium," she said cordially. But beneath that fluffy white professional persona, I detected sadism, ill-concealed glee in beholding the suffering of another human being.

I poured a large paper cup full of the stuff, tilted it back, took a large gulp, and nearly fell off the table. It was not the taste so much. It was the way the stuff felt in my mouth. Now, even months after the episode, I can still feel it in my mouth. Did you ever drink mint-flavored motor oil laced with chalk? Gag. Heave. But I drank it down. Then another and another and another. After a few minutes I lost track. I became convinced they had given me Elijah's pitcher of cooking oil; the more I drank, the more it mysteriously re-filled itself.

Finally, the pitcher empty, I stumbled toward the large table and made ready to lie down. From somewhere, the technician reappeared.

"You've got one more cup to drink. The pitcher does not hold quite enough."

My quivering insides nearly exploded in open revolt. But I took it and managed to get most of it down. With an inch or so remaining in the bottom of the cup, I handed it back to the technician. "Unless you want to clean up me and this room, you better flush the rest of this stuff. I cannot drink one more swallow."

She gave me a "Gee, what a wimp!" look, but she took the cup and disappeared toward the rest room.

The CAT scan is a big machine that can make a series of detailed pictures of areas inside the body. The pictures are created by a computer linked to an x-ray machine. The patient lies on a table with arms over head. When the picture making begins, the table moves through a large, round, doughnut-shaped camera that scans the whole body.

Full of barium, I tried to make myself comfortable in preparation for the filming process. But the sinister technicians were not through with me. In came a nice-enough-looking young man. "Mr. Maddox, in order to get a full scan, we've got to put a tube up inside of you through which we will inject some more barium. You will experience a warm sensation for a few seconds as it moves through you. Don't be alarmed."

Sure, don't be alarmed with a six-inch water main invading your rectum. He poked something small inside me. Actually, it was so small I hardly felt it. And sure enough, very quickly, from my waist down, I felt a warm sensation. Weird.

After a few more minutes of that kind of organized torture, the technician announced he was through. I should go to the rest room and get rid of the barium. I could then get dressed. They would give Dr. Regan the pictures, and he would be in touch with me.

> **Looking back on the tests, I realize I did not suffer any pain.**

It felt great to get off that table, feel that stuff leaving my racked and torn body, put on my clothes, and get out of the radiology lab.

Looking back on the tests, I realize I did not suffer any pain more than a twinge here and there. To their credit, the technicians tried to tell me every move they intended to make. I was just not prepared for all the intrusions. It might have helped for them to take another minute or two to explain more thoroughly their methods and what I might experience.

But maybe no amount of conversation would have equipped me to deal with all the fluids, feelings, injections, sensations, jabs, and jostlings.

Would I go through it again? Yes. The idea of doctors groping around inside of me with uninformed hands holds no charm, to be sure. I would rather they have the test information to guide their probing. Face it: Not many of us welcome the tyranny of technology over our bodies in a time of illness, but I have not come up with a better solution.

The Blood Bank

Next stop, the Red Cross Blood Bank at the hospital. When I asked about the presence of the Red Cross in the hospital, the receptionist explained, "We run this unit on a contract basis with Georgetown University Hospital. Why should the hospital hire and train a blood-bank staff when the Red Cross has a group of skilled experts available?" Made sense to me.

Through the years, I have given many units of blood, so donating blood held no particular terror for me. During some of my years as a minister in Georgia, I actually headed up the local blood drive.

AIDS has dramatically changed the way blood is collected, managed, and distributed. In the 1970s, when the bloodmobile came to our local National Guard Armory for the quarterly drive, donors did not have to sign multiple forms or ask themselves one more time if they had had intercourse recently with a person of the same sex, used a dirty needle, or for some other reasons did not want their blood used by another human. I do not recall the nurses using rubber gloves as they touched donors. Today's professionals take every precaution to protect their own safety as well as the integrity of the national blood supply. But do they ever pry!

After interminable forms and more "have you ever . . . ?" questions, the nurse began drawing my blood.

"What in the world is 'autologous donation'?" I asked her.

"That's when you give blood for your own use," she said, with just a slight hint of "Where have you been for the last hundred years?" in her voice.

The next week I returned for a second run—but with some unexpected side effects. The nurse who put the needle into my arm missed the vein and had to fish around under the skin to make the proper connection. Her fishing did not hurt terribly, but the idea that she was wiggling a long, sharp needle in my arm had its downside.

"Your arm might become slightly discolored from my probing," she warned.

"Okay," I replied weakly.

After several agonizingly long seconds, she hit her mark, and the donation began to move ahead. "Squeeze on the little knob in your hand every few seconds," she instructed, then turned to sign in another patient. She kept checking to make sure all proceeded properly. After about twenty minutes, she gave me the welcome word: "Just about done. A few more seconds."

She extracted the needle, put a puff of gauze over the hole, then told me to push hard against it with my other hand and keep the arm elevated.

Old stuff, but it felt different this time. In just a few seconds, I could not see the end of my arm! My eyes clouded over. Sweat popped out on my face. I began to float to never-

never land. *Would I die in the blood bank? Was this the end of a beautiful life?*

The nurse noticed my rapidly deteriorating condition. "Mr. Maddox, you're not doing great right now, are you?" she asked, her voice coming from Pluto or somewhere. "Just lie real still. I'll get you some cold compresses. You're having a neurogenic reaction to the donation. Probably triggered by the probing I had to do to get your vein. You'll be okay in a few minutes. You can lie here as long as necessary."

One of the forms I had signed before giving blood said the hospital would supply emergency treatment if necessary. I began to listen for the intercom to scream out some kind of Code Red for me, but nothing happened.

A half-hour later, with several cold compresses on my head and neck, skillfully administered by the nurse, I began to approach land again. The dark dizziness lifted from my eyes. My stomach calmed down. I slowly sat up, hung my legs over the side of the table, and remained very still. No way. Not yet. Lie back down. Two more waits and two more tries, and finally I felt I could make it to the goody table for some juice and cookies. It took me a full hour to recover and trust myself enough to leave the blood bank and head for the parking lot.

What had gone wrong? My wife and secretary diagnosed that I had pushed myself too much. Two harrowing, life-threatening tests, then giving two units of blood, complete with a nurse making a pincushion of my arm. Together we reached a management decision: I would wait two weeks before giving that last unit of blood.

My third trip to the blood bank went without a hitch. As I started to leave, the nurse gave me some forms. "Take these with you to surgery," she said. "Do not give them to anyone ahead of time. Make sure someone in authority gets them. These papers establish that you have given blood, where it is, and that it is yours to use."

I clung to those forms for dear life, stashing them in the glove compartment of my car so I would run no risk of leaving them at home on the *big day.*

The Final Consultation

About ten days before surgery, Linda and I went to Dr. Regan's office for the final consultation. He could not have been more helpful or understanding. He was frank, yet positive, as he laid out the options before me:

- watchful waiting
- radiation therapy—several variations
- cryotherapy—a largely experimental approach that freezes the cancer cells
- hormone therapy
- radical prostatectomy

Watchful Waiting

I could choose to do nothing. Sometimes a tumor like mine could remain practically dormant for a long time or, at worst, grow quite slowly. By keeping it under close observation, engaging in what the trade calls "watchful waiting," I might avoid surgery for a long time.

Radiation Therapy

I could go through a regimen of radiation that would probably reduce the tumor; it certainly would impede its growth.There are two main methods for conducting radiation therapy, external-beam and radioactive seed implants.

In external-beam radiation therapy, doctors beam radiation from outside the body on the diseased area. Radiation therapy does damage some strong, healthy cells, but cancer cells are more susceptible to the high-energy beams; they die, while healthy cells have more resilience. The body has a way of replenishing those healthy cells that succumb to the powers of radiation-beam therapy. Today's highly trained radiologists, with the sophisticated technology available, can use radiation quite efficiently, posing little overall danger to the patient.

Radiation seed implants, or interstitial radiotherapy, involves surgically placing tiny, rice-size radioactive pellets into the cancerous prostate. In the best-case scenario, the pellets kill cancer cells without requiring the seven to ten weeks called for by radiation-beam therapy. Research indicates that, whereas seed implants require less time to work than the beam protocol, this treatment often falls short in providing the desired long-term results. Some experts even go so far as to label seed implants as ineffective.

Most doctors will explain that radiation therapy is not an acceptable treatment for virulent, aggressive cancer. If radiation does not work, removal of the prostate becomes all the more risky. In fact, Dr. Regan suggested he probably would not attempt to remove my prostate if I took the radiation route and did not achieve the desired results.

What's more, radiation treatment for a man my age could have side effects akin to those resulting from surgery, with far less assurance of long-lasting success. I remembered, with a shudder, the effects of radiation on my father in the early 1970s. The radiation that bombarded my father's lower back for six weeks or more turned his skin to leather and made him terribly nauseated. Dr. Regan assured me that to-day's procedures had long passed such a primitive stage. Even so, he did not want me to go that route and neither did I.

Cryotherapy

Cryotherapy, or cryosurgical ablation, involves the con-trolled freezing of the prostate. Dr. Regan pointed out that this is still a relatively experimental technique designed to kill the cancer cells. Though it has promise, he said that its effectiveness as a long-term treatment is still uncertain.

Hormone Therapy

Hormone therapy seeks to eliminate male hormones from the body, the most common of which is testosterone. Certain hormones, particularly testosterone, promote cancer growth. When the troublesome hormones are eliminated from the body, cancer generally stops growing. It may even go into remission.

Not everyone is a candidate for such an approach. It is usually reserved for men whose cancer has broken out of the prostate and therefore is not amenable to surgical removal.

Radical Prostatectomy

Finally, I asked, "What do you think I should do?" Without a blink, Dr. Regan told me a man my age (fifty-seven at the time), in general good health, with a family history of pros-tate cancer, should have a radical prostatectomy—that is, have the prostate removed, accompanied by a concomitant examination of related lymph nodes.

"Even with such an operation, I cannot promise you will never have another problem with cancer relating to the prostate. But in my opinion the probability drops to almost nil. You can adjust to the changes in your life. We are steadily improving our approaches in dealing with incontinence and impotence. I would be completely surprised if you have long-lasting effect from incontinence. We will work with you on the impotence."

Because of my persistent concern about impotence, I asked him about sparing the nerves that control erection. He assured me he would do everything he could to avoid cutting those nerves, but he could promise me nothing. (In a lengthy conversation some months after the surgery, Dr. Regan said he did avoid cutting the important nerves, though it would still take time for them to be restored—and even then maybe not entirely. More on that later.)

Using posters, Dr. Regan explained the surgery to Linda and me. He proposed removing the entire prostate rather than simply going for the lesion, to ensure he got all the cancer. He would have to cut one of the sphincter muscles that helped control the bladder, but he could leave the other one undisturbed. I should not have any long-term effects of the loss of bladder control.

He would have to sever the urethra tube from the bladder, cut away the diseased prostate, then reattach the urinary tube to the bladder. Because of this, I would have to come home with a catheter. I should plan to keep it in place for two to three weeks following the operation.

He suggested an epidural anesthesia rather than a general anesthesia for the surgery. "I do not want you talking to me during the operation," he said lightly, "but if we can avoid putting you all the way under, it's better. You come out easier."

"Dr. Regan," I quickly replied, "pain is not my best thing,

neither physical nor emotional. I have no need to coach you through the operation. An epidural is okay if you say so, but I don't want to know a thing about what you're doing."

He laughed but caught my drift. "You won't know much about what we're doing." He went on to explain that an epidural anesthesia puts the patient way down in sleep but is less stressful than a general dose of the good stuff.

He projected a hospital stay of five to seven days. In light of today's very short hospital stays, I found that stunning in itself. They were going to put me through the medical wringer, for sure.

The operation would be no picnic, but he anticipated no surprises. He wanted me to lose all the weight I could and build up some more stamina by walking.

Shaken but fairly secure, Linda and I prepared to leave the doctor's office. As Dr. Regan shook my hand, he said, "Mr. Maddox, the grace of God brought you in here at the right time. He'll see you through this."

A skilled doctor fortified by strong faith . . . what more could I ask?

Over the next few days Linda and I intensified our efforts to get ready for the surgery. We talked a great deal about what lay ahead. We did our share of grieving over lost opportunities to strengthen our lives together during the past few years. We both purposed to open ourselves even more to each other in the next weeks as this drama unfolded in our lives.

Prostate Homework

During those days of decision making (and since), I read extensively about diseases of the prostate.

In the December 15, 1995, *Washington Post,* Dr. Thomas A. Stamey of Stanford University School of Medicine noted that prostate cancer "presents the individual patient, his physician and the overall health care system with a serious dilemma." The main reason, says Dr. Stamey, is that prostate cancer tends to strike later in life and grow slowly. Breast cancer tumors double every three or four months. Prostate cancer tumors typically take three or four years to double. That means prostate cancer poses little threat to men who get it late in life. In fact, most experts agree that dramatic treatment in older men could present more problems than the disease.

> **Prostate cancer poses little threat to men who get it late in life.**

The number of radical prostatectomies done in American hospitals has continued to soar, doubling from about 50,000 in 1991 to 100,000 in 1993. Stamey says as many as half of those operations are either unnecessary (because the cancer is too small) or ineffective (because the cancer has already spread beyond the prostate).

Stamey suggests that few, if any, men over seventy should receive aggressive treatment for prostate cancer because half of them will die of natural causes before they reach eighty-two, the average life expectancy of a man of seventy. For a man over seventy—"Unless he comes in with his father," one doctor joked—he would perform no surgery and undertake no dramatic treatment.

In younger men, even a slow-growing tumor may have time to spread and become deadly. Once the cancer has moved outside the prostate, medical science can offer no definitive cure. Patients who have a life expectancy of ten years or more after diagnosis should be treated with either surgery or radiation, the experts generally agree.

In November 1995, Washington, D.C.'s mayor Marion Barry announced he had prostate cancer. In conjunction with his announcement, an eleven-member panel of experts said they could not declare one treatment clearly superior to others. The panel evaluated three treatments: radical prostatectomy, radiation, and watchful waiting. The panel avoided a definitive recommendation.

In subsequent reading I learned that some doctors have striven to develop techniques that avoid severing crucial nerves, leaving patients with the ability to have natural erections after radical prostate surgery. These same doctors, however, point out that prostate cancer tends to colonize in many parts of the gland, not all of them obvious. If the surgeon steers clear of those critical nerves, some hidden cancer cells may remain.

In a lengthy "Health" section article in the May 23, 1995, *Washington Post,* Patrick Walsh, the chief urologist at Baltimore's Johns Hopkins University, who pioneered the nerve-sparing surgery, said men should remember that the most important goal of prostate surgery is to eliminate cancer, since most recurrences ultimately prove fatal. Indeed, Walsh ranks sexual potency as third in importance, after complete removal of the cancer cells and careful repair of the urethra to maintain urinary continence.

Frankly, from my own experience, from talking with other men who have had similar operations, and from rather extensive reading, it is evident that the problem of impotence has not been conquered. Research points to hope, but for the most part we are not there yet.

The incidence of incontinence, impotence, and cancer recurrence after prostate surgery varies from survey to survey. A summary of side effects prepared by the Office of Technology Assessment, entitled "The Prostate," came up with the figure of 85 percent impotence after a radical prostatectomy, the surgery Dr. Regan recommended. If the surgeon can spare the critical nerves, impotence drops to something like 30 percent. External-beam radiation pointed toward 42 percent impotence but with a much higher risk of recurrence of the cancer.

The same summary showed much more promise dealing with incontinence. Only 7 percent reported serious problems after the radical surgery, with only 1 percent after radiation. Approximately half of the men surveyed routinely use absorbent pads or clamps.

Other studies reveal different, more positive results. The most important statistic is that 70 to 90 percent of the patients remained cancer-free ten years after surgery in cases where the original cancer apparently was confined to the prostate.

> **Seventy to 90 percent of the patients remained cancer-free ten years after surgery.**

The Preadmittance Routine

Because of restrictions on the length of hospital stays, most surgical procedures call for the patient to come to some sort of preadmit unit several days ahead. Gone is that army of volunteer pink ladies and men who met the patients at two in the afternoon the day before the surgery and smartly wheeled them up to their room. The testing, blood work, and routine chest x-ray take place in this preadmit phase under the patient's own steam.

For me, the preadmit came one afternoon a week ahead of time. When I arrived at the Georgetown AM Admit Unit, the secretary completed the essential data, including the insurance information, then handed me off to nurses who began a round of probing, picking, sticking, listening, and history taking. Efficient, competent, alert to medical nuances that might affect the operation, they made a serious effort to personalize the visit. I could almost hear hospital public-relations officers warning the preadmit folks to make the patients feel welcome.

Waiting for the next technician to drop in on me, I noticed the elderly woman in the curtained-off cubbyhole next to me. For all the world, she looked like Mrs. Doubtfire in her body suit. The staff must have been in the process of preparing her for a procedure that afternoon from the way they were giving her the once-over. To my amazement, she seemed excited at the prospect. She talked with glee about her problems with gas after surgery, what kind of food she wanted, what medicines did and did not work with her. Whatever was about to happen to her was making her day. *Lord, fill up my life with more than pains and operations.*

As my preadmit episode began to draw to a close, the nurse told me I should report back to that same suite at six thirty the morning of my surgery.

"Don't bring anything with you," she advised. "You'll get shuffled about considerably before you finally arrive at your room. Have your wife leave your necessities in the car until you get fully settled." I knew the litany about nothing to eat or drink after midnight the day before the operation. What smacked me hard, filled me with dread, was *the jug*.

"Mr. Maddox, a full twenty-four hours before your surgery, finish filling this gallon jug with water; then place it in the refrigerator so it can chill. You can see that it only contains a small quantity of liquid. This is Golytely. Starting at three o'clock on the afternoon before your surgery, begin drinking it. A large cupful every half-hour. It will gently clean out your system. It's not harsh. And it doesn't taste all that bad if you chill it. Once you start the Golytely, do not eat any more solid food. It's essential that you let this stuff work. Okay? Any questions? Have a nice day."

A gallon! I have never drunk that much of anything in such a short time. *It doesn't taste all that bad.* Ha!

Countdown

The following days both dragged and flew by. Linda and I could not seem to stop all our doing and going long enough to talk about what was happening. We both dreaded the ordeal. Neither of us could predict the short- and long-term ramifications of the operation.

The weekend before, we fed thirty college students at our house, members of a touring choir in which Elizabeth, our daughter, sang. Sunday, church. Monday, a last push to gather up details, pay bills, and make yet more essential preparations. By Tuesday afternoon, the clan began to gather into what became a somber but important celebration of family.

I am the oldest in my family. Scattered along behind me are three more brothers—Mike and the twins, David and

Donald. Though we have all endured our share of life's twisters, we have remained close. It moved me deeply that they would make such a special and costly effort to be with Linda and me. Ben, our second son, and Andy, our oldest son, with his son, Will, "Number One Grandson," rounded out the dinner table. Elizabeth would return from her choir tour late in the evening.

We laughed, joked, prayed, and cried, with me excusing myself periodically to respond to the demands made by that gallon of Golytely.

Suddenly, it was bedtime. Never have I so not wanted an evening to end! I had no fear of dying on the operating table, but I did mortally, everlastingly dread what lay ahead for Linda and me. During my illness she would have to pick up an even heavier load.

Lord, into your hands . . .

Chapter 7

The Surgery

I jumped straight up in the bed when I turned over and saw the little red numbers blinking on the digital clock by my head. "Oh no," I moaned. "We must have had a power failure in the night. I've missed my appointment at the hospital!" Bounding out of bed—and jarring Linda from her sleep—I raced to the den to look at the battery-operated wall clock. 4:00 A.M. Whew! Saved. If I had not stirred, looked at the clock, and realized the problem, I could have missed the appointment.

We went back to bed and dozed fitfully until 5:30 A.M.. We had to make it to the hospital by 6:30. After stumbling through the process of getting dressed, my brothers, Linda, and I huddled on the sun porch for a prayer and another round of hugs before driving to Georgetown Medical Center.

At 6:15, the May sun had already begun its climb into the eastern sky. Already legions of people had squirreled themselves away in the nooks and crannies of hundreds of office buildings, plotting strategies, making deals, flattering and cajoling and spending public money in even greater volumes than the Potomac's flow. As I eased the car into the hospital parking lot, I felt gratitude to George Washington and all the others who laid the foundation of this city. If I had to have my insides ingloriously invaded, I was glad to have it done in such a glorious setting. Might as well do it in style.

I thought we would have the place to ourselves, but I missed that one by a mile. From the looks on the faces of those scattered around the waiting room, a dozen or more people seemed to share my state of anxiety. Their families had the same visage of dread on their faces as did mine. Misery loves company.

Someone called my name. I hugged my brothers one more time, and Linda and I headed

My brothers, Linda, and I huddled on the sun porch for a prayer and another round of hugs.

back into the curtained recesses of the unit. With chart in hand, a neat, friendly nurse attached the name and ID tag to my wrist.

"You are Mr. Robert Maddox, aren't you?" she asked. To make sure, she had me recite my Social Security number, the name of my doctor, and my home address. I could not help wondering if they ever make mistakes in this place—take out some guy's gallbladder when they were aiming for his prostate? I hoped not.

Then came the inevitable.

"Please take off all your clothes and put on these hospital

gowns. For now, you can put on two, front and back. But I have to tell you: once you get back into surgery, they will remove the one from your backside." I silently complied. Linda gathered up my stuff and placed it all in a white hospital-supplied plastic bag.

Next, Nurse Nightingale fitted those incredibly tight white surgical stockings on my legs, but with an added twist. "These will breathe for your legs," she said. "Once you are in your room, the staff will attach them to a small pump that will inflate and deflate these little pouches, diminishing the possibility of a blood clot forming in your legs."

Gowns and stockings in place, I sat down with Linda for a minute. She hugged me one more time, told me she loved me, that I would be fine. I told her I loved her, not to worry about me, that I would be all right. We commended each other to the Lord and prepared even further for what lay immediately ahead.

A young man with a gurney pulled the curtain back. "Mr. Maddox, time to go."

I had read accounts and seen movies of people walking stalwartly up the scaffold steps, staring the hangman in the face, while the muffled drums beat their doleful cadence. For all the world, I felt like that. Here I was, about to be wheeled into the buzz saw. I knew pain and suffering awaited me. I had no choice but to go.

With a final kiss and hug from Linda, a pat and handshake from my brothers, I disappeared down the hall.

Poked, Prodded, and Panicked

I was on no medication, yet I felt sedated, floating, as the man rolled me through the twists and turns of the hospital labyrinth. In a few minutes, we stopped. Several faces peered down at me, including Dr. Regan's.

"Mr. Maddox, you are in the best of hands. Dr. Vinakayom and his staff will handle the anesthesia. They are tops. I'll see you in a few minutes."

With that, I looked into the face of a distinguished man in his middle fifties who spoke with an Indian accent. "We plan to give you an epidural anesthesia," he carefully explained. "We then will place a small catheter in your back between two of your vertebrae. It will remain in place for several days after your surgery and will be the primary way we control the postoperative pain. In fact, you will be your own pain-relief manager using a device that we will demonstrate to you a bit later on."

They had me sit up on the side of the gurney. Someone rolled a tray apparatus up to my head and told me to lean my head over onto the tray. "We want to stretch your spine a bit so we can place the injection at just the right spot in your back."

Then the antimalpractice litany kicked in.

"You should know and agree that this procedure can cause severe headaches and back pain. Do you agree to the procedure?"

My psyche cried out, "No, I don't want any of this!" But I meekly nodded my head in the affirmative.

The doctor's resident, a young woman, spoke next. "I'm going to palpate your back to open the right space for the injection." With that, she began to slap my backbone.

Suddenly, as she slapped my back, as doctors and technicians poked at me while talking about *Oprah* and God knows what else, a new emotion roared through me, one I had never known before despite two other surgeries. My whole being cried out, "Run! Get away from this. Maddox, you cannot stand another second of this medical trash. Your body is going to jump off this cart!"

I physically gripped the tray, ready to leap. Then, mercifully, I began to drift.

"There," the resident exclaimed with a note of triumph. "It's in place. We will start the anesthesia running. When the operation begins, you will hardly know anything."

More panic, despite the floating.

"Listen, Doctor," I slurred, "I don't want to know a frapping thing about this operation. I told Dr. Regan I wanted to be out entirely. Don't leave me hanging. Do whatever you have to do, but I do not want to be awake at all!"

"Oh, I see," he said, a note of quiet surprise in his voice. "Open your mouth. Let me look inside."

I complied.

"Hmm, we've got a bit of a problem," he observed. "Nothing we can't take care of, but I am glad you told me of your strong feelings. After we get you into the operating room, we may have to place a device in your throat. Don't be alarmed. Everything is under control."

Actually, by then I did not have a care in the world.

They rolled me into the operating room. I recall the big overhead lights, the slide from the gurney to the operating table, Dr. Regan's masked face looking down at me. At some point, the anesthesiologist leaned over me and said, "We will have to put this instrument in your mouth. Please open wide." And then nothing else.

Life in the Twilight Zone

Several lifetimes later I began to come back to earth in the recovery room. I looked around and saw other patients in various stages of waking up.

"Tell me your name," a nurse said.

I told her.

My body had no feeling, yet I felt absolutely awful. I knew where I was. I knew what had happened. Yet I was not there, either.

"You did just fine," the nurse assured me. "No problems. We've told your family you are here. After a while, when you wake up some more, we'll take you to your room." I don't remember the move. I just know that, at some point, they rolled me into a room.

"Mr. Maddox, you've got to help us get you from the stretcher to your bed. Slide right on over," a voice from space instructed me.

I mindlessly obeyed and fell away into sleep for a few minutes.

When I opened my eyes, Linda, my brothers, our friend Molly, and others were standing around the bed.

"You've done great," Linda said. "Dr. Regan told us everything looked just right. No problems."

"Good," I grunted through parched lips. "Can I have something to drink? My mouth is so dry," I mumbled.

"I'll ask the nurse," Molly said.

In a blink she was back. "No, you can't have anything to drink for a while. You've got to wake up first."

Groan.

At some point I became terribly nauseated. With nothing in my stomach thanks to the Golytely action, I had the dry heaves. They lasted for hours.

Andy brought my grandson Will into the room for a few minutes. I remember seeing him sitting across the room, his big brown eyes looking at me. While he sat there I had another spell of heaving. Later, Andy told me, Will came out of the room saying, "Granddaddy went . . . " and made a heaving sound like he had heard me making. When everyone laughed at him for his extraordinary cleverness and perceptiveness, the heaving sounds became the brilliant kid's number one act for the rest of the day. I regret that I missed it. Probably his stint in my room shaped his future, sent him on a trajectory to Harvard Medical School, then on to a Nobel Prize in urological research.

Time meant nothing.

My back hurt.

My mouth screamed for water. All they would do was wet a little sponge swab and swish it over my lips.

Night came. Members of the family left, but Linda stayed all night, sleeping on a cot by my bed. She was wonderful. I would rouse up, needing her. She would pop off the bed, tend to my needs, then fall back into sleep.

I recall little of that night except the comfort I felt in knowing she was in the room with me. I also had wonderful nurses, though I do not remember what they looked like.

By morning, the nausea had subsided, but still they would give me nothing to drink.

"Your system has not waked up yet. You wouldn't be able to handle anything in your stomach. You would get sick again. With the anesthesia wearing off, heaving would hurt like crazy," one of the nurses warned me. I would remain in a state of screaming thirst. Lawrence of Arabia had nothing on me.

Sometime during my life in the twilight zone, one of the nurses came into the room, announcing, "You've got to get up and sit in the chair."

I had read about lunatic hospital people, and now I had met one in the flesh. This woman put the Wicked Witch to shame. "You've got to be joking," I moaned. "I can't move, much less get up and sit in a chair. Look at all these tubes and drains."

"I'll be back in a few minutes to bathe you, change your bed, and help you get into the chair." With that, she mounted her broom and swept out of the door, cackling her frightful laugh.

When she did not return immediately, my psyche celebrated: "They got rid of her before she seriously hurt somebody."

But no. After a while she returned, bearing a load of clean sheets and towels. Then, rather than bathing me herself, she put a little plastic tub on my nightstand, gave me the washcloth and towels, and firmly told me to do my own bath. What about all that TLC nurses dispensed? Bathe myself.

I have to admit it did feel good to stir around, to take the sponge bath. The warm water and rough cloth made me feel halfway alive again. Two nurses helped me turn on my side so they could sponge my tormented back and check the epidural shunt. After just a few minutes of this strenuous, if refreshing, exercise, I lay back utterly exhausted.

> **The warm water and rough cloth made me feel halfway alive again.**

"Now, we get you up."

"I really do not think I can do this," I pleaded.

"Yes, you can. You have to."

They cranked up the head of the bed, helped me get my right arm under me, gave me a pull, eased my feet over the edge of the bed, and aimed them for the floor. Despite the pain, I managed to slide into the reclining chair they had pulled up to the bed.

I must have collapsed into the chair and fallen asleep because I do not remember anything else for a while. Later, I learned that, in the midst of this shuffling around, Dr. Regan had sent word he wanted me moved to another region of the hospital where I could receive more direct urological care. I did not want to move. After all, the new nurses might abuse my torn and bleeding body even more than the current crop. Besides, despite their sadistic streak, I had grown accustomed to these folks. In the final analysis, however, given my precarious condition, geography concerned me not at all. I just did not want to be hurt anymore.

I recall looking out into the hall and seeing a big, black, straight-backed wheelchair parked by my door. One of the nurses told Linda, "His room on the other floor is not ready, and the patient is waiting for this room. We'll just wheel him out into the hall and let him wait there until his room is ready."

To that bit of news Linda replied, after a moment to collect herself, "No, I don't think we'll do that. We're paying for a room, not a hall." That settled that! I would have cheered, but I figured it would hurt too much.

When the time came for me to move, rather than putting me in the wheelchair, the wonderful nurses simply rolled me in the recliner. Somehow we maneuvered the halls and elevators and made it to the new room. I endured the painful process of going from chair to bed; then I promptly passed out into blissful oblivion.

Assessing the Damage

As I began to come out from under the anesthesia more fully, I could be a bit more analytical. For starters, I got a glimpse of the incision—wicked.

They had cut from my belly button to the pubic bone, then stapled me back together again. On either side of the incision, they had inserted drains—tubes running deep inside my body attached to plastic bubbles about the size of lemons. Periodically a nurse would come in, yank the sheet down, expose me in all my glory, and empty those little lemons. After a time or two, when I saw the nurse come into the room, I saved her the trouble and flung the sheet aside myself. Modesty? Long gone.

The epidural shunt remained in my back, but it caused me no discomfort. I still do not know how they had inserted it, where it stuck, and why it did not bother me, but so be it. Once a day, someone from the anti-pain department—to the tune of $139 a pop—examined the system to make sure it continued to function properly.

A tube from the epidural shunt ran up my back, across my right shoulder, and into a device about the size of an audio cassette. That gadget, a pain-controlled analgesia (PCA for those of us who now understand medical lingo), contained the pain medicine along with a button for me to push when I needed a fresh infusion of relief. According to my own pain needs, I could push the PCA button and release a carefully measured dose of medicine into my back. The staff proudly explained this device with care, as if showing off yet another new medical toy. They had programmed the device in such a way that I could not overdose, even if I wanted to.

It worked, especially after I caught on. Early in the process I found myself hurting, could not figure out what to do, and then it would dawn on me: push the button, stupid. Ah, blessed relief.

Of course I had an IV running because I had still not had anything to eat or drink. My system simply would not wake up sufficiently for me to tolerate any sort of food or drink. Frankly, I did not want anything to eat, but I surely did crave something liquid to ease my parched lips and terribly dry throat.

And then there was the catheter, a ball and chain that would become my companion for the next three weeks. (More on that later.)

By the afternoon of the second day, I settled into something of a routine and made ready to spend the next several days in the hospital. I did not puzzle over my fate, gave no regard to how long I would remain in the place. I lost track of time, did not read the newspaper, could not have cared less about world affairs.

It surprised me to feel the world rolling on as if nothing had happened when, in fact, the operation of the century had occurred. But the world's not-knowing did not weigh heavily on me. I focused instead on just getting to feel better. On living, despite the staggering odds I was sure I faced.

Chapter 8

The Hospital Stay

Dr. Regan had told me to anticipate several days in the hospital. I assured Linda and the clan I would definitely come out on the short side of the equation. No way would I stay there for a whole week.

I missed that one, big time.

I had the surgery on a Wednesday. They moved me to my new room on Thursday. I hardly remember any of that day and night. By Friday morning I felt myself gradually coming alive again. I felt bad, terrible—but I was regaining some control over my life.

They had yet to give me anything to eat or drink. Food, I did not want. But I yearned mightily for something to drink.

"Your system still has to wake up," one of the residents told me. "We did a great deal inside you and had to put you deep into sleep. If you start eating or drinking too quickly, you will have big trouble." So I had to content myself with dabbing the little spongy swab at my parched lips and swishing it around in my fevered mouth.

During early rounds that Friday morning, another resident

asked me if I had passed any gas, as he poked around on my wounded stomach.

"No, but so what?"

"Well, passing gas is a sure sign your system is returning to normal. You cannot eat or drink anything until you begin to pass some gas."

Something else to look forward to.

Later in the day, Linda and Molly came to check on me. "How are you feeling?" they inquired.

How does it look like I'm feeling? I thought. I mumbled, "Better, I think."

"Do you need anything?" Molly asked.

"Yes, I need gas. I may die of thirst if I do not soon pass some."

They thought I was joking. I did not laugh. I was not trying to make a joke; all I wanted was to make gas. If that was the only way to get something to drink, I wanted to get on with it. I was thirsty.

Then, on Saturday afternoon, it happened! It started as a pronounced rumbling in my stomach, moved around for a while, swelled, subsided, then rumbled some more. No stranger to the special male propensity for breaking wind, I recognized the

> **I wanted to get on with it. I was thirsty.**

sensation. I felt a new thrill. Maybe this was it. *Oh, gullet,* I invoked, *make my day.* And it did. In the quiet of my own room, comforted by the loving attention of my family, assured of the skill of the medical staff, I passed gas! I would live again!

Triumphantly, I snuggled down in my sheets, gave the pain pump a healthy nudge, and dozed off into contented sleep, lulled even more by the gratifying rumble of my insides as gas passed and passed and passed.

Liquid Ecstasy

The next morning, I told my doctor about my success. But he would order nothing for me to drink until he had checked with the nurse. Naturally, I had informed her during the night of my overarching achievement, and she had dutifully noted it on my chart.

"Mr. Maddox, you can have some apple juice," the doctor reported back. "I'll order it." I wanted to grab him by the knees and say, *"Bless you!"* But since I could not get out of bed, I had to content myself with a heartfelt "Thanks!"

As soon as the doctor left the room, I pushed the call button to order my juice! I waited. I imagined how it would taste floating down my emaciated throat. I waited. I would savor it, pour it over ice. I waited. I would sip the wonderful elixir in a delirium of ecstasy.

But the nurse would not come. I buzzed her again. "I need my juice," I admonished the voice at the other end.

Finally, a vision in white came into my room, bearing a small tray. I raised up in bed and ignored the searing pain, the better to see and grasp the treasure. My hands trembled as I reached for the precious liquid. To my dismay, I saw nothing that looked like a drink. I quickly put on my glasses. Maybe my eyes were not focusing yet. The glasses helped. I saw on the tray a tiny medicine cup of apple juice.

I nearly wept. "That's all I get after five days in the medical desert? I have done everything you told me to do. I have passed gas. For days I have lingered at the brink of dehydration only swabbing out my mouth with those dratted little swabs. And now, you come in here with a double tablespoon of juice!"

If I could have managed it, I would have turned away, hid my face in the pillow, and sobbed. But of course I took the juice. "Please bring me a cup with some ice in it," I requested. I carefully poured the smidgen of juice over the ice, swished it around to make a tiny apple-juice freezie, and carefully sipped. Absolutely delicious. Never in my life had anything tasted so good. Watching the liquid disappear, I savored every drop. For maybe half an hour I nursed my life-giving potion, feeling its wonderful properties flow through my body. *Ah, sweet mystery of life, at last I've found you.*

A Good Meal Gone Bad

Sunday night the doctor let me have a liquid diet—some kind of clear broth extracted from wildebeest horns or blue heron eggs, gelatin the consistency of putty, runny ice cream, and hot tea. I tried, but I could not manage to eat much of what was on my tray. One look at it took away what little appetite I had worked up.

Monday morning, I did better. Still a liquid diet, but this time they gave me something that faintly resembled Cream of Wheat. I nibbled at the mush and ate half of a half piece of last week's toast. I wanted coffee but had to content myself with the hot tea. Progress.

During rounds that morning, Dr. Perez, Dr. Regan's assistant, told me he would give me a better diet for lunch. I was doing fine, he said. Time for me to try some real food.

I sat up in a chair most of the morning. A dear friend came to see me, bringing me the latest John Grisham book. She and I had a wonderful talk about the church, friendships, and the goodness of God. After her just-right visit, I even felt well enough to work on the manuscript for this book. Then, at noon, the kitchen delivered lunch.

With keen anticipation, I whisked the lid off the huge tray and beheld food—real food—in abundance. Creamed potatoes, coleslaw, bread, Jell-O, and barbecued spareribs! For me? I glanced at the ticket that came with the tray: "Maddox. Room 313." It was for me. Wow!

Still sitting in the chair despite some of the tubes sticking in me, I began gingerly to eat my lunch. I tasted the creamed potatoes. Okay. With growing confidence I took a bite or two of the coleslaw. No problem. With knife and fork in hand, I pulled off a healthy chunk of the ribs and popped it into my mouth. Good. Quite tasty. Another bite or two of the coleslaw, and then I was full. Better not push my luck.

Since I always take my plate to the sink after eating at home, I tidied up the tray and put the cover back on the dishes just to help out the dietitian when she came back in. Feeling tired and just a bit uncomfortable, I managed to crawl back in bed unassisted, though with considerable effort. I stretched out, planning to take a quick after-lunch nap, feeling proud and grateful for my good progress. I must have dozed off for a few minutes.

I awoke with searing pain. On my right side, near my lung, I had a deep, gripping pain. Turning on my side did no good. Thinking that getting up might help, I lumbered out of bed, put on my robe, hooked my catheter bag to the rolling pole that held my IV, and pushed out into the hall. By that point, I already knew every inch of that hall but purposed to endure its monotony yet another time if only my agony would subside. Up and down I trudged, leaning on and pushing the IV pole ahead of me. Agony!

Desperate, I called the nurse. "You've got to help me," I lamented. "This pain up in my right side is about to kill me. It's as bad or worse than anything I have experienced so far."

Nurses do not like unexplained pain in their patients. She listened to my stomach, chest, and side. She poked around a few times. "Mmm," she murmured. "Let me get you a different kind of pain pill, something mild but strong enough to help. The doctor has something on your chart," she muttered, more to herself than to me.

Thirty minutes later, the pain had not abated.

Then her nurse's intuition kicked in. "What did you eat for lunch?"

"The doctor gave me a regular diet."

"What was on your tray?"

"Not much. Creamed potatoes, Jell-O, bread, coleslaw, and barbecued ribs."

"Coleslaw and barbecued ribs! You're not serious! From nothing to cabbage and pork? I should have looked at your tray. I would never have let you eat that kind of food. I'm sorry. You're having severe gastric pains."

Immediately she brought me some Mylanta. I wolfed it down. But nothing happened.

Then she got really serious. "Just to be sure it's not anything else, I want to do a cardiogram."

She rolled in her machine with its newfangled self-stick electrodes to which she attached the familiar wires.

About that time, Linda walked in and nearly had a heart attack herself. We had talked that morning, and I had felt wonderful. Then, when the pains set in, I had tried to call her, but I could not focus sufficiently on my quirky phone to get the call to go through, so she had had no warning of my distress.

"What's the matter?" she asked in a panic. "What's happened to him? He was fine this morning. Is he having a heart attack?"

The nurse, my favorite of several good ones, hastened to assure Linda I had no signs of an attack, but I was having considerable pain that nothing seemed to ease. Just to be sure, she was going through a check list ruling out possibilities. "I called the doctor, and he has ordered some x-rays, just to make sure he's not having gallbladder trouble."

That was the first I had heard of gallbladder trouble. In a flash I could see myself careening through the halls toward the OR for yet more surgery.

But the x-rays revealed nothing. Gas. Coleslaw and barbecued ribs dumped into a trembling, fragile system simply proved too much. Life-threatening maladies ruled out, Nurse Wonderful gave me a shot of something that put me away for the rest of the evening and much of the night. The next morning, with fear and trembling, I peeped at my breakfast tray. Grits and soft scrambled eggs. With extreme caution I put a few bites in my hesitant mouth, pushed the rest aside, and lay back to see what would happen. Nothing happened. The best *nothing* I had known in a long time.

Report from the Operating Room

At some point during those $1,500-a-day experiences, Dr. Vinakayom, my anesthesiologist, appeared at the foot of the bed.

"Mr. Maddox, you did very well in surgery. We encountered no unexpected problems," he reported. "I do, however, need to give you a word of caution for any future surgery you might have." With that he began to describe a weird throat construction I have of which I had been totally unaware. As he talked, I remembered him taking special note of the construction of my throat when I told him I did not want to know anything about Dr. Regan's cutting. It seems that my air passage can present a problem during surgery if the doctors are not fully aware of how I am built in there. Under certain conditions, my air passage could become closed, posing serious dangers.

"Should you need any further surgery," he went on, "be sure to tell the doctor of my findings. By doing so, you will avert possible serious complications."

What had the doctors actually done to me? Later, I asked Dr. Regan that very question.

They had performed a retropubic radical prostatectomy. This begins with an incision from the navel to the pubic bone. Because the prostate is located behind the pubic bone, it is necessary to make a large enough entry cut to work in that confining space. Then the diseased gland has to be carefully separated from everything else holding it in place. The surgeon separates the urethra from the bladder, removes the damaged tissue, then reattaches the tube to the bladder without its cozy thumb-and-blanket prostate gland—hence the necessity for the catheter and its aggravating bag while the vital healing and rebounding take place.

In the surgery, sphincter muscles that enable bladder control take a beating. In fact, one gets cut away entirely, putting all the responsibility on the remaining muscle and creating the problem of incontinence. Neighboring lymph nodes are removed to make sure the cancer cells have not spread into them.

Also, in the process, certain nerves that assist the penis in having an erection get damaged—not severed, but dramatically tinkered with. That is why it takes some time for sexual function to be restored. Of course, sexual feelings do not go away, just physical ability. And only for a while, the good doctor assured me.

On their way out of the body, the doctors insert those little drain tubes I had seen, so the excess fluids that build up in the region of the operation can get out without causing infection.

Once all their cutting and walking around inside the body is complete, the doctors make like carpenters, stapling the two sides of the gaping wound together.

No wonder I felt so bad when I began to come around. The body snatchers had really done a number on me. Time to heal, that is what I needed. Thank God, I had the time, and I did heal.

Long, Long Nights

Nights in the hospital can get terribly long, especially in that no man's land between the zonked-out condition right after surgery and the time when the body begins to function with some measure of normality. The second, third, and fourth nights lasted a year each. About the time I would settle into a decent sleep, the night nurse would come in to check me over. On popped the light. Down swished the sheet. Squeeze went the lemon bottles on either side of my incision. Temperature. Blood pressure.

I would try the television, thinking perhaps CNN would

lull me to sleep. The hospital did not have cable. Besides, the television exerted a definite negative effect on me. For some reason, I could not take it for more than a few minutes at a time. Eventually, I gave up on it entirely.

Then another condition began to plague me. I would drift off to sleep only to be punched awake by some sort of body reflex. About the third morning, I mentioned my strange sensation to the doctor.

"You're having bladder spasms," he quickly surmised. "Happens all the time with this kind of surgery. I'll give you something."

The pill worked. No more spasms.

I have taken very few sleeping pills in my life. Rather than working as described, they put me right on the brink of sleep, in a maddening kind of spirit world. After three nights of restlessness in the hospital, however, against my better judgment, I took the sleeping pill the nurse offered. Within a few minutes I kicked out—but not far enough. I never saw elephants on the ceiling, but talk about bad dreams!

Getting through the Days

Visitors were a mixed blessing. What would we do without visitors? And, to be sure, what do we do with some of them? I learned to dread those who come in with their knitting needles and picnic basket, prepared to keep the patient company for the rest of the afternoon. Then there is the guy whose friend had this same operation. "Course, he died from a raging staph infection the third day. But, hey, you're lookin' great!"

I needed my family—Linda and our son and daughter,

Ben and Elizabeth, were fantastic. Our friends Molly and Walt and others knew exactly when to come, what to say, and how long to stay. I needed their assurance and friendship. I received lots of cards, beautiful flowers, and some thoughtful get-well gifts.

I unplugged the telephone. I am not much for the phone anyway, even when I am well. If the family came in and they wanted to plug it in, fine. But when they left, I disconnected the dratted thing. On the rarest of occasions the charge nurse would buzz me to say I had an important call coming in, would I please turn on my phone? I did, answered the call, then yanked the plug out of the wall again. Later, several people told me they had tried to call but could not get an answer. "Yeah, I know," I said.

Coughing is another challenge to patients mending after surgery. Oh, how it hurts to cough or sneeze! Before I went into the hospital, my uncle called to urge me to have the nurses make me a "coughing pillow." That is good advice. Lying flat on my back, as much as I tried to avoid it, I would have to cough or, even worse, sneeze sometimes. After a time or two of that unbelievable pain, I followed my uncle's counsel. To my surprise, the nurses knew exactly what I needed. They wrapped tape tightly around a couple of small pillows and presented them to me complete with a marker inscription: *Bob's Sneeze Pillow.* Then, when I needed to cough or sneeze, I pressed the pillow firmly against the weak muscles of my abdomen. Believe me, it helped.

Walking is the best medicine for coughing. But did it ever hurt the first few times I had to get out of the bed and walk. If I thought I would expire when the nurse first had me sit up in the chair the morning after surgery, when she told me, on the second day after the Mother of Operations, that I would have to walk, I tried to become comatose. She would not relent; I was to take up my tubes, bubbles, bags and walk. Then she said, "If you walk, you will stop coughing. Your lungs need the exercise."

Walking is the best medicine for coughing.

That did it. Despite my precious little pillow, coughing and sneezing were inflicting the agony of the damned on me. Walking could not be half as bad as coughing.

My first doubled-over, clinging-to-Linda-and-the-IV-pole trip took me only to the door of the room. I was cheered as if I had run the Marine Marathon. Later in the day, the nurse came back saying, "Okay, you've got to walk some more. This time, push yourself out into the hall. Go as far as you can."

Same procedure, but a tiny bit easier. The hall disappeared into infinity. Never have I seen such a long, long corridor. I made it about halfway, this time hanging on to the wall rail with my left hand and leaning on the rolling IV pole with my right. The next time I made it down the hall and back—a trip I could now manage, since they had miraculously shortened it during the night.

Soon, the entire enterprise was a piece of cake. Three or four times a day I hauled out of bed without any assistance, got all my paraphernalia organized, and moved out into the hall for several laps, gradually straightening up more and more. As a result, the coughing stopped. My lungs began to work better, though I still could not take truly deep breaths, despite huffing and puffing into the plastic breathalator, a clever device the hospital supplies to surgical patients to stimulate the lungs and stave off pneumonia. (By the way, when I started to leave the hospital, I left the breathalator on the table. The orderly who was wheeling me to the car said, "Mr. Maddox, you just paid nearly thirty dollars for that. You might want to take it home with you.")

Finally, the hospital staff removed the tubes. Out came one of the drain bubbles. Next they took away the pain device. Soon, they freed me from the IV drip. The day before I went home, Dr. Perez snipped the staples that held my body together. The next day, they pulled out the last drain bubble and tube. It stung like a low-voltage electric shock when it came out, and I was surprised at the length of the drain tube—about twelve inches.

The Power of a Little Cross

I have heard horror stories about hospital staffs. Even though I had my moments with the folks on my floor, looking back I fully realize they wanted only to do their job—and do it well—with me in mind. So they took a while to get my juice, made me bathe myself, and had me sit up and walk months before I felt ready. I did well under their care. I sing their praises.

Georgetown University and Medical Center exist as an arm of the Roman Catholic Jesuit order. As silent yet eloquent testimony to that religious connection, every patient room has a small crucifix on the wall facing the bed. I had some interesting and, I pray, productive conversations with the Christ of that tiny cross, particularly during some of those long nights.

As I have already mentioned, I entered the hospital with a plate full of problems. At the tender age of fifty-seven, I had done a great deal of living and left my share of debris in my wake. My overriding commitment had long been to serve the Christ represented by the crucifix. I had, however, surely lost sight of that commitment in more than a few instances.

> **Those year-long nights pushed me to some honest, often painful assessments.**

Those yearlong nights, looking at the cross, pushed me to some honest, often painful assessments. I had much for which to be grateful: wife, children, daughter-in-law, grandchildren, friends, substantive ministries. But I also had to wrestle with the mistakes, missteps, and outright sins of inattention, carelessness, tossed-away opportunities, selfishness, and stubbornness against God and others. I came to a fresher sense of the presence of God. I came to a clearer notion of what I needed to be about, coupled with an urgency to get on with it. That wonderful, freeing grace of God I cherished dawned on me in a way like the Kellogg's Corn Flakes ad slogan, "Try them again for the first time." Over and over I have seen that about the time I think I understand the grace of God, some new dimension of that wonderful spiritual commodity pops up before me. *Thanks, Lord, for the surprises.*

Perhaps the biggest piece of good news and bad news that oozed into my brain as the IVs oozed into my body had to do with forgiveness. Long ago I had begun to grab hold of the Christian doctrine of forgiveness with a vengeance. Believe me, I like that one. I firmly believe God in Christ has forgiven me of my sins. No amount of "good works" can earn me that eternally "Paid in Full" chit. Fine. No problem. Relief. I need not lug around a great load of guilt feelings. That is grace in spades.

In the hospital that little crucifix reminded me of some reading I had done a long time ago. Dietrich Bonhoeffer and Robert Clyde Johnson both talked about the cost of grace and forgiveness. While I do not have to feel guilty for my sins forever, I can never erase the guilt for some of the things I have done. The effects of my actions remain in my family, in other people, and, in a larger sense, in society. So I have to take responsibility for that guilt while learning to release the feeling of guilt. That makes a lot of sense to me. Tough, but possible.

To keep forgiveness in perspective, Johnson wrote in *The Meaning of Christ,* "What God offers us is not good-natured indulgence of our sin, but costly forgiveness." For me, costly forgiveness means getting my act together. Taking greater responsibility for my actions. Pushing through my fears, inhibitions, pride, and hardheadedness to clean up some messes I have left.

Did I receive comfort from that cross? Not especially. Did I sleep better because of its presence? No, but it did help lead me to new resolve, hope, determination to make some important, and of course difficult, changes. Old habits die hard. In a perverse way they seem like old friends, comfortable to be around and not too challenging. *O Christ of the Cross, continue to shove grace my way and, if you will, generate a new surge of courage to get me back, for real, on the path where I belong. Do not be done with me yet, please, Sir.*

Chapter 9

The Road to Recuperation

On the seventh day after the operation, a resident came into my room with an announcement: I could probably go home if I felt like it and wanted to.

A wave of panic swept over me. I was not sure I wanted to leave my warm womb and tackle the real world. Besides, I did not feel great. The terrible episode with the barbecued ribs had racked me less than eighteen hours before. What if that happened to me again? I might actually die before getting back to the hospital.

Who would look after me? Linda, Elizabeth, and Ben had their own lives to live. Linda, especially, had all she could say grace over. I could picture how they would pile me down on the bed, hand me a tin of chicken noodle soup and the can opener, and leave me to fend for myself. Before I knew it, they would expect me to make my own bed, empty the dishwasher, fold clothes, brew the morning coffee, maybe even empty trash cans. Was I ready for such a world? No way. I needed to stay a few more days. I had two insurance policies that would cover the expense. *Doctor, why don't you just leave me alone for another week or two?*

I slid down in the sheets. I made a point not to buzz the nurse at all that day. Like a good boy, I ate most of my bland lunch, walked without any assistance, straightened up my bed, threw away the newspapers, and kept very quiet.

> **Was I ready for the real world?**

Good News from a Cloud of White Coats

Preliminary reports from the surgery had all looked good. Dr. Regan assured us that, to the best of his knowledge, the operation had removed all the cancerous tissue. He had experienced no surprises, and everything looked fine. He cautioned, however, that he would not know for sure until a lab had conducted a thorough examination of the tissues, a process that would take a few more days. Linda and I did not fret too much over the possibility of bad news from those extra tests; still, the concerns lingered. Then, in the middle of the afternoon on that day the resident had told me I might go home, I looked up, and in came a cloud of white-coated human beings, most of them total strangers. *Uh-oh*, I thought. *Something is about to happen.*

"Mr. Maddox, I'm Dr. Lynch. These are my associates. We work with Dr. Regan. I saw you in the operating room, but you probably do not remember me."

No, I did not.

"We've received the full report from the labs . . ."

Yes, yes, go on, you sadist! my mind screamed.

". . . and everything is fine! We have no indications of

any further trouble. We believe the operation was a complete success. You should not need any further treatment whatsoever, though we will want to see you every three months for the foreseeable future. By the way," he added as he turned to leave, "the tumor was larger than we had expected, and it was a bit nearer breaking out of the prostate than we had imagined. You are a lucky man to have caught this early as you did. Good luck."

What a wonderfully warm and caring doctor is this guy in the long coat! Tremendous bedside manner. Completely competent.

"You will need to see Dr. Regan in about two weeks so he can remove the catheter. In the meantime, if you have questions or concerns, do not hesitate to give us a call," the kindly, brilliant Dr. Kildare informed me. Then the entire medical corps did neat about-faces and trooped out, chatting among themselves as they left. No more word about going home today. Typical absent-minded geniuses, they had forgotten such a mundane detail as my dismissal.

The afternoon wore on. I dozed. Walked. Arranged and rearranged my bed. I attempted to prepare my body/stomach for whatever mystery meat would lurk beneath the cover of my dinner tray.

About five o'clock, my neat, dependable world crashed in on me. In zipped one of the younger residents. "Mr. Maddox, you feel like going home, don't you? You've done so well. No need for you to stay another day. You know, the expense, and all that."

"Well, I don't feel just great, Doctor. I'm still uneasy about what I can eat. It's okay with me if I stay until tomorrow. Besides, my wife is not here. She would have to come in through all the traffic."

He did not budge.

"Why don't you give her a call. See if she can get here. Meanwhile, I will sign your discharge orders. We'll see that you have all the equipment you need. The nurse has given you instructions on the catheter. You can take showers when you get home, but do not get into the tub until after you see Dr. Regan in a couple of weeks. We don't want any water getting up into the catheter."

With that, he shook my hand warmly and left the room. Rats!

I called Linda, and, of course, she dropped everything and came after me in a hurry.

As I waited for her to arrive, I heartily thanked God the tumor had not broken out of the prostate and begun its lethal trek through my blood and bones. Dr. Lynch's words had given me a jolt. What if the cancer had broken out? On the basis of Dr. Regan's assurances, we had never seriously contemplated such a possibility.

The Right Treatment

What does happen to those men whose tumor has "broken out," as Dr. Lynch had said? All my research indicated that once the cancer begins to move around, it cannot be definitively cured. That is what had happened to my father. Lack of knowledge and inattention to the problem had set him up for seven years of discomfort, uncertainty, and, ultimately, his early death. But subsequent reading and several conversations with doctors helped me understand that in many cases loose prostate cancer, though not "curable," is not necessarily a death sentence.

Treatments are available. However, most doctors seem to

agree that if a patient's prostate cancer has spread—and thus is inoperable—the question of the right treatment can prove quite difficult.

Loose prostate cancer is not necessarily a death sentence.

Some doctors say that unless some form of treatment has a more-than-reasonable possibility of helping the situation, the patient should ignore the fact that he has a potentially lethal disease. He should just go on with life as if everything were fine. For many of us, though, it is impossible to ignore the alien spreading through our bodies.

When we think of ways to fight back at cancer, our minds almost immediately turn to chemotherapy. While many cancers do respond to various chemotherapy protocols, my research indicates it is not the standard treatment for inoperable prostate cancer. Depending on the stage of cancer and its location in the body, some form of radiation or hormone therapy has proven more productive. Even these do not anticipate a 100 percent cure, but they have been helpful in impeding the growth and further spread of the cancer.

In some instances and in some geographic locations, you might be eligible to participate in an experimental study. Talk with your doctor, contact a cancer-treatment facility, or call one of the several cancer-research centers to see what might be available. New treatments come along steadily. If you read about one, discuss it with your doctor or others in the medical profession.

If you or someone you know bumps into the tough problem of treatment, talk openly with your doctor. Your physician wants you to have the best quality of life possible. Then get some other opinions. When you are ready, you and your doctor can decide which way to go with treatment.

The Only Real Cure

During my years as a pastor, I have often related to people with a disease that does not yield readily to acceptable treatments. Some of these patients have gone off on expensive searches for exotic cures. I urge extreme caution before you invest time, hope, and resources trotting around the globe seeking these "spectacular" remedies. They are invariably quite costly and may do no permanent good.

When my father's cancer was declared inoperable and proved quite aggressive, he and his doctor tried everything to forestall his death. He had radiation. He took drugs. He had an orchiectomy—that is, he had his testicles surgically removed, hoping to slow down the production of testosterone. As the cancer cells invaded his bone marrow, he was transfused with massive amounts of blood platelets—all to no avail. He died from what the doctors called radiation sickness and cancer of the bone marrow.

This less-than-glowing appraisal of treatments for prostate cancer that has spread prompts me to sing my same song again: Go early and often to your urologist for screening. Men over forty with a family or racial propensity for prostate cancer should have regular examinations. All men over fifty need to see the doctor annually. Early detection is the only real cure for prostate cancer.

At Home, with Catheter

I really did not want to leave the hospital. I wanted to be home again, but I did not want to leave.

Later I came to understand why some folks like hospitals. Patients do not have to assume much personal responsibility there, just move along with the routine. Food shows up. So do fresh towels, clean gowns, attentive personnel, flowers, nice cards, and a new book or magazine from time to time. No bills to pay, no garbage to get down to the street, no family hassles to adjudicate. No need to fret about what the president is doing or why the Supreme Court ruled as it did in that big case.

Despite my wishes, by six o'clock that last day, my week in the hospital was disappearing in the rearview mirror. Two helpers had showed up at the room with carts and a wheel-chair. We had loaded up the flowers and plants, the hospital stuff I had paid for, a couple extra gowns the nurse sent along, two catheter kits, the breathing machine, and some pajamas I had never worn, and then we trundled it all down to the car. Driving with extreme caution through the heavy traffic, Linda got me home safe and sound, if terribly exhausted. I piled down on the couch in the den, a site that would become almost the sum total of my territory for the next ten days.

The doctor had told me all along that I would go home with the catheter in place. Ugh! A day or so before they dismissed me, the day nurse spent a few minutes training me in the use and care of the bag and pushed me to manage it for myself before leaving the hospital. I quickly learned its intricacies, how to flush it from time to time, how to change it, and especially how to position it so I could get around. If I wanted to walk up and down the hall, I hooked the catheter to the IV pole; then, after the nurses disconnected the IV drip, I simply picked up my bag and walked.

The catheter never hurt. I could not forget its presence, but it did not give me any physical discomfort. The emotional discomfort is another story. I hated the feeling of being tethered, of having to do with a ball and chain. When I complained about having to stay in the house for those weeks, the hospital staff showed me how to wear a leg device so I could step outside if I wanted to. As my training with the bag was drawing to a close, however, the instructor said, rather offhandedly, "By the way, if you sit too long with the bag on your leg, the drainage tube can back up, run over, or flow up inside you." With that charming piece of news, the very idea of going anywhere with the leg bag struck terror.

After my first week at home, some members of the church called to say they wanted to drop by for a visit. I hurried around, changed the arrangement, put on long pajamas in place of my trusty hospital gown and rather bedraggled bathrobe, then tried to sit prim and proper while my friends and I chatted. I kept surreptitiously casting my eyes downward, not knowing what to expect leaking from my nether regions. The minute they left, I yanked off the leg job, tossed it in the trash, and, feeling like I was welcoming an old friend back home after a long sojourn, reattached my trusty bag.

Life in the Living Room

I discovered the first night at home that I could not get comfortable in the bed. Because of the incision and the catheter, I could not sleep on my side without props. Finally

I hit on the idea of moving to the couch in the den. Ah, sweet relief. I curled myself into position between the seat cushions and the sofa back and hung my bag onto the cross supports of a TV tray, building myself a nest that made for fairly comfortable sleep.

I had quietly determined to make the best of my three weeks or so of enforced convalescence. Never in my adult life had I been required to sit still for such a long time. At first, I could not focus on much more than television. I tried reading and writing, but my mind would not get into gear. Quickly, however, the fog began to lift.

I wanted to make considerable progress on this book. I had started it before I went to the hospital and thought about it often during the ordeal, and I had even made one feeble attempt at note making while residing at the Georgetown "Hilton."

At first, my efforts at writing were frustrated because I could not find a way to sit and write. I tried putting pillows in the dining-room chair. Too hard. I put my laptop on a TV tray drawn up to a Queen Anne chair. The angles were not right, and every movement caused me stinging pain from the lower regions. Then, I came upon it. By placing my laptop in my lap—how about that for genius deductions— while sitting on the sofa, I could move right along. From then on, every day, I could work on the book, write letters. As time went along, and when I grew strong enough to return to the pulpit, I prepared worship services and sermons. In fact, this new site for laptop production has stayed with me.

The living-room sofa became my office. Initially, Linda and Elizabeth tried to get me to find another place for all my stuff, but they soon gave up. At about the time I thought they might arrive home from work, I would pile up my mess in more or less orderly stacks—keeping all my working notes, documents, books, mail, and junk nearby so I would not have to trek through the house gathering them together while dragging my bag along with me. Amazingly enough, I got a great deal of work done without taxing the body too much. If I felt myself getting especially tired, I stretched out on my trusty couch. Every day, of course, I took a nap.

At first, just about the time I got fixed in a comfortable position, the phone would ring, and I would make a grab for it. Quickly I worked out a system with the family. If they called and I did not answer, they should call right back if they needed me, and I would pick up. I even got to the point where I could unplug the closest phone extension and let another phone out of earshot pick up any messages. No longer am I a complete slave to the telephone.

In my convalescence I was not a slave to work either, even if *work* meant simply typing a letter.

With all I have to do on a regular basis, reading good stuff for pleasure has always stirred up a wave of guilt. *You really do not have time to enjoy this extraordinary book,* a voice deep within chatters into my soul's ear. During this time I resisted the voice and indulged. In three weeks I put away four wonderful books: two classics, a splendid work of historical fiction, and a beach novel with no real redeeming value other than its being fun to read. I also found a new pleasure in reading the Bible—not with an eye on next Sunday's sermon preparation, but for my own enrichment. Highly productive.

Throughout those days at home, the mail carrier brought a daily stack of get-well cards. Friends dropped by with food and good wishes. Phone calls assured me of prayers and abiding interest. And my family provided incredible support.

The Weight Thing

I had gone into the hospital packing too much weight. I determined to use the occasion of the surgery as an opportunity to lose some of the excess baggage around my waist, and I did.

One disconcerting aspect of the weight battle occurred during my time in the hospital. After about three days of no food whatsoever, feeling sure I had lost thirty or forty pounds, I stepped on the scales. To my dismay, not only had I not lost any weight, I had gained about five pounds. Embarrassed at first, I did not ask anyone about my condition. Finally, I told the nurse she ought to junk those scales because there was no way they could be right. She laughed and told me my problem related to all the fluids they were pouring into me. Once I got off the IV, I would quickly shed the water. Exactly.

Within a few days after my return home, those fluids fled my body via my bag, and I saw my weight steadily decline. It has not gone away as rapidly as I wanted it to, but my eating has fundamentally changed. We have almost eliminated the fatty foods that provided the backbone of the Deep South menus on which we were reared. Like never before we pay attention to fat content and all those other tables on the packages of the foods we eat. I figured it would take me a year of this kind of attention to get my weight down to the range where it ought to be, but I would get there. This time next year, my friends would not recognize me, I promised.

Working My Way Back

The fourth Sunday after surgery, I returned to the pulpit for the first time, free of the catheter and eager to realize a goal I had set for myself. The doctor had given his approval, but he also predicted that I would feel mighty washed out if I made it through the service. He had that right. I could hardly wait to get back home and collapse in the bed. Still, it felt mighty good to be on the move again. Life.

Little things happened that stand out above my accomplishment in being able to return.

About midway through the week prior to that first sermon after the ordeal, I received a call from one of the young men in the church on whom I have come to rely heavily.

"Bob," Doug said, "you'll need help Sunday morning in the pulpit. You can't do it all, no matter how good you feel. So I've decided to conduct most of the service. You give me the order of worship, and I'll figure out my part." I did not argue with him.

The service went well despite the breakdown in the air-conditioning equipment. The members welcomed me back with open arms. They likewise sent me home in a hurry. "You head home," they said. "We'll take care of everything here." I did and they did.

I stayed away from the office all that week, but I did lead the next Sunday's service, even managing to go out to lunch with some of the folks. Of course, the bed reached out and grabbed me when I stumbled back into the house.

The doctor had suggested I not drive for a full six weeks, the only order he gave me on which I fudged. I did not take unnecessary chances, but a time or two after three weeks at home, emergencies arose that demanded I get behind the wheel for short runs. I felt uneasy, lest I have a fender bender that could wreak havoc on my operation, but nothing happened.

The fourth week after surgery I began to keep limited office hours. No one need to have worried about over-extending. By midday I had spent myself and limped home to the couch or to the bed. Fortunately I could make good use of home computers, printers, and the telephone, so my work and other responsibilities did not suffer too much.

I feel for people whose work suffers from extended illness. Thanks to a generous congregation, I received a paycheck the entire time I convalesced; my pay was not directly dependent on my labor. That measure of freedom facilitated my recovery. Salespeople and hourly employees would certainly face great stress in a time of illness such as I experienced. Unless a person had disability coverage or a good nest egg, recovery could prove an uphill financial struggle. In fact, many might be tempted to put off surgery in the first place because of their inability to deal with the lost income.

The Plumbing Situation

On schedule, I returned to Dr. Regan's office two weeks after returning home and three weeks after the operation (our thirty-fifth wedding anniversary, by coincidence). For the trip, I wore a pair of short pants, both for comfort and to accommodate my catheter. I honestly felt like a schoolkid, so excited was I with the prospect of getting rid of my ball and chain.

One of Dr. Regan's nurses took me into the examining room, sat me down on the edge of the table, took a look at the arrangement, and began making some adjustments to the equipment.

"You've got a bubble up inside you that has kept the tube

from sliding out. This little valve allows me to deflate the bubble." Deftly she twisted a tiny cap.

"Now," she said, "count to three and hold your breath."

Clever lady. As I began to count, with my mind on what would happen when I held my breath, she "detubed" me with one smooth motion. It stung for a second with that electric-like shock I had felt when the doctors removed the drains in my side. Then it was over. "Free at last, thank God, free at last!"

But not quite.

The doctor had told me to expect some measure of incontinence. In preparation for that visit to the doctor, Linda had bought me a package of pads I could insert in my underwear as protection against the drips. That same clever nurse who had removed the catheter gave me a moment's instruction on the use of the pads and described some exercises I could use to strengthen my bladder control. She called them Kegel exercises. Later, my daughter told me her friends use the same exercise so they can have better sex. Did I ever begin to exercise!

Each man has a different experience with incontinence following prostate surgery. According to press reports, General Norman Schwarzkopf, who had surgery the same day I did, said he had no trouble with incontinence and indicated he had little with impotence. That bothered me for a while because I had trouble with both. Then it dawned on me: Of course he had no trouble. His system would

> **Each man's experience is different.**

not dare defy the general! No self-respecting bladder or erection-controlling nerve would come up against a man as formidable as Schwarzkopf. The reports also suggested he took off for a bout of fishing just a few days after the operation, while the rest of us mortals had to lie around in our ratty housecoats and hospital gowns with embarrassing tubes protruding from our bodies for at least a couple of weeks. Oh well, that is why he led the charge into the Gulf War while I watched it on CNN.

For the first several weeks, I had to change pads several times a day. I had a horror of having an episode that would call undue attention to myself. That never happened, but I did experience a persistent leak. Anytime I left the house, I made sure I had a few pads tucked away in my briefcase. As I steadily gained my strength, the drips receded.

My family and a few of our closest friends, especially some of the young men in our church, knew of the plumbing problems that persisted. You would think their pastor could get more respect. But no. They never failed to hold me up to friendly ridicule and shame.

"Don't forget your Depends," they would taunt.

Still, I sooner would have left my American Express card at home than go anywhere without my pads.

As I recovered, we took a couple of trips. Naturally, I stuffed the side pockets of my suitcase with just-in-case pads. A year and a half later, while unpacking from yet another trip, I felt a lump in the deeper recesses of my favorite suitcase. Feeling around, I came up with three or four rather mangled but still usable pads, reminders of days gone by.

On one of those early postoperation trips, I began to notice increased problems with the drips. Though I had no pain or discomfort, I became sufficiently alarmed to call Dr. Regan's office from Texas.

Upon hearing me explain my problem, the nurse immediately opined, "Since you're on vacation, I bet you're drinking more coffee and colas—too much caffeine. Cut down or drop caffeine drinks entirely for a few days. You'll probably clear up promptly." I complied, and within a day my condition returned to normal. These many months later, if I seem to have more-than-usual incontinence, I pull back on the caffeine with surprisingly favorable results.

This talk of incontinence leads me to an interesting sidebar story. I had surgery in late May. By early August my incontinence had all but gone away. I could go all day long without any significant problems, yet I still did not feel at ease leaving home without one pad somewhere nearby. I always slept with one in my underwear, just in case.

Linda and even Elizabeth began gently to say, "How's the drips?"

I could honestly assure them the problem was much better but that I still depended on Depends. Then Linda suggested, "Maybe you do not need them at night." Finally, it dawned on me she might be right. One night I took the plunge. No protection. And no problem. In a few more days I realized I could manage fine without any help at all.

A conversation with a friend also helped. To my surprise, when talking with him one day several months after the surgery, I learned that he had had prostate-cancer surgery several years before. We talked frankly about the surgery's hangovers.

He told me that his incontinence went away, almost. Like me, he had worn some sort of protection for a while but then stopped.

"Bob," he said, "it's been three years, and I can still have a small problem if I sneeze, cough, laugh, or turn a certain way. But not enough to cause any embarrassment. I'm the only one who ever knows about such episodes."

If incontinence persists, talk with your doctor. She or he may have a few medical tricks to suggest. Certain drugs can help tighten the muscles that control urination. A clamp device is also available, but doctors seem reluctant to employ it, especially for a long period of time. While some problems afflict all patients for a while, if you have serious, prolonged incontinence, go to the doctor. Do not suffer in silence.

Chapter 10
Recovery, Retooling, and Restoration

Recovery from prostate-cancer surgery lies along a continuum. You do not suddenly wake up six weeks and three days after surgery to find all systems go. Just as every man is different, and every incident of prostate cancer is slightly different, the process of recovery, retooling, and restoration varies from person to person. In fact, the more men I talked with, the more convinced I became that we need as much education about recovery as we do about the condition of prostate cancer itself. Men with excellent training in their own fields—ministry, military, trades, crafts, etc.—come up distressingly uninformed about the processes of recovery. I also have to fault the medical profession for not better informing men about the ups and downs of retooling. Fortunately, my team at Georgetown University Medical Center has taken considerable time coaching me on how to get back up to speed.

To help me and others understand recovery more completely, I interviewed several men to get a clearer under-standing of their experience with prostate cancer and treat-ment, and to talk about their present condition, especially in relation to incontinence and impotence, the two most com-mon lingering residues. In all instances, the men have given me permission to use their sto-ries, though I have changed their names. They have encour-aged me to let other men know the dangers of prostate cancer and the routes to recovery.

> **The process of recovery varies from person to person.**

Tom's Story

Tom served twenty-five years in the military and retired a few years ago with high rank. He does not recall precisely when he began having urinary troubles, but the problems became noticeable in 1993. He found himself getting up several times in the night with an urge to urinate, only to find he could not make a stream.

He told his fiancée of his problems.

"What do you intend to do about it?" she asked.

"Oh, I'll watch it for a time. I'm sure it will get better," he replied, attempting nonchalance. "Actually," he later told me, "I was about fifty-five at the time, and I guess I thought such aggravations went with age. I did not like to get up in the night, but since I was having no pain and the problem did not seem to bother me during the day, I was prepared to dismiss the whole issue."

When the problem did not go away, his fiancée, herself

a military nurse, told Tom one day, "I made an appointment for you with a doctor at the military clinic."

The first doctor Tom saw did not think the problem was serious. "He told me to watch the situation. He may have given me some pills; I don't recall. I was to come back if I did not get better soon. Well, I did not get better, so I went back and asked the doctor to examine me more closely." This time the doctor got serious. He had Tom conduct a urine flow test—that is, urinate in a container periodically to help the doctor evaluate Tom's system.

Then the doctor performed a digital rectal exam and discovered a hard spot on the prostate. At that same time, the doctor drew blood for a PSA test. The PSA came back at 3.0—not alarming, but high enough to bear watching. After a week or ten days, Tom, following the doctor's orders, returned for a cystoscopic examination of his bladder. Nothing of moment showed up in Tom's bladder.

Finally, after several weeks with Tom traveling back and forth to the clinic, his doctor decided to perform the transrectal ultrasound and biopsy. The biopsy revealed the presence of cancer. The Armed Forces Institute of Pathology confirmed the diagnosis.

The clinic doctor sent Tom to a urologist at Walter Reed Army Medical Center in Washington, D.C. There Tom was retested and had a bone scan. When the Walter Reed urologist had his facts together, he informed Tom that he definitely had prostate cancer—probably low grade, slow growing, probably still contained in the gland, but malignant.

In assessing his options, Tom decided to have a radical prostatectomy as the surest way to remove the danger. He opted to have the surgery performed at Bethesda Naval Hospital in suburban Maryland. The surgical protocol at the Navy hospital called for a perineal operation; that is, the incision was made between the scrotum and the rectum.

Tom remained in the hospital for four days administering his own pain medicine with the PCA pump. "I had very little pain in the hospital, but I did have severe pain for several days after I went home. The incision did not bother me; I felt bad pain up inside me. I had to take pain pills regularly for several days."

Like every other prostate-cancer-surgery patient, he left the hospital "bag in tow." The Bethesda doctors removed it twelve days after surgery.

"I wore diapers for several weeks after the surgery. I never actually flooded, but I surely did drip constantly. Gradually, I began to exchange the diapers for pads. I guess I had resigned myself to permanent incontinence. Then, suddenly, while I was out of town on a trip, about three months after the surgery, practically full control returned. I did not need any extra protection from that time on."

Tom does say, however, that he can still drip. "If I get emotionally upset," he says, "I can have trouble. Seems that my bladder and my emotions are closely connected. Anger, frustration, and uncertainty seem to increase incontinence. It's not enough to make me wear extra protection but enough to notice." An excessive amount of caffeine increases the drips.

Tom continues to have problems with impotence. The last time he and I had a serious conversation, I mentioned to him the various therapies available. He seemed surprised to learn of the possibilities and indicated he would talk with his doctor right away.

Sam's Story

Sam is a minister who has spent his career serving as a chaplain with some key national institutions. In 1992, when he was sixty, during a routine physical the doctor gave him a rectal examination to check his prostate. Everything seemed fine. But the doctor said, "With age creeping up on you, let's give you the PSA blood test."

Sam thought nothing else about it until a few days later when his doctor called. "Sam, when you get a chance, drop by the office. We need to talk."

With just a bit of anxiety, Sam detoured by the physician's office on his way home that afternoon, noting to himself that doctors always give you good news over the telephone but want to see you face to face when they have bad news.

"Your PSA is slightly elevated," his doctor said. "It may mean nothing at all, but this is a reliable test. I found nothing unusual when I felt your prostate, but sometimes problems do not show up in a way that a doctor can feel until it's too late. I'd like to do some more tests just to be sure." After the round of Trans-Rectal Ultrasound examinations and biopsies, sure enough, they found that Sam had prostate cancer in its earliest, most contained stages.

The doctor offered him the standard choices: watchful waiting, radiation, or surgery. As a surgical option, the doctor said he could remove only the diseased part of the prostate, but he did not recommend such a limited procedure.

Sam, a friend of many in high places, recalls, "The first person I called after my wife was Senator Bob Dole. The senator had recently faced the same situation and had opted for complete removal. 'Come to my office,' the senator invited. So I went. In that moment Bob Dole became my minister. He listened intently. Understood thoroughly. Encouraged me with his prayers and support and assured me I was going to be all right. I will never forget his genuine concern and willingness to help me over the initial shock."

Next Sam called a physician friend at the Mayo Clinic. "If you want to," Sam's friend offered, "have your doctor fax me his findings. I'll be glad to consult with him if that will make you feel any better." Sam's doctor readily complied.

In a few days the Mayo Clinic doctor called to say he agreed with Sam's physician. When Sam asked his friend, "What would you do if you were in my shoes?" his friend said, "Sam, I'd have the surgery."

Still, Sam was not satisfied.

In talking with a physician son-in-law, Sam pleaded, "Tell me the name of the best radiologist you know in the area."

The radiologist, just to make sure, did the ultrasound test again. "You can undergo radiation with a reasonable expectation of success," the radiologist concluded. "We have made many advances. The treatment is not nearly as debilitating as it was only a few years ago. You probably will not be sick. You should not lose any hair, certainly not on your head."

Then Sam put the question to the radiologist: "What would you do if you were me?"

Without any hesitation, the doctor said, "I would have the surgery. At your age, with the tumor no more advanced than it is, I would not take any chances. I'd have the gland removed."

So he did.

After a seven-day stay in the hospital, Sam and his catheter went home.

Sam's recovery curve was steadily upward. He soon felt better and was steadily regaining his strength. During convalescence he had no special pain other than general discomfort. His incontinence gradually ceased. Today, more than four years after surgery, Sam plays handball and other sports. "Occasionally, if I pound the floor especially hard, I can have the drips, but never enough for it to show through my clothing. I'm careful about drinking too much coffee, though I have not gone entirely to decaffeinated drinks."

The impotence? "That was the last to clear up," says Sam, who has been married more than forty years. "Now, I'm almost back to normal. It's never quite the same, but it's all right."

"By the way," he chortled, "tell your readers they don't have to have an erection to feel good or to have happy times with their partners. Takes a bit of extra doing, but the loss of a prostate gland does not necessarily ring down the curtain on sexual intimacy."

> **The loss of a prostate gland does not ring down the curtain on sexual intimacy.**

Like every other recovering prostate-cancer patient, Sam was told by his doctor, "Come back every three to six months for a checkup and a PSA."

At the appointed time for yet another PSA rerun, Sam stuck out his arm for the technician to draw the requisite vial of blood, then went on about his business.

Then came the phone call from the doctor: "Can you drop by my office?"

Oh no! Not again, Sam moaned inwardly.

"Sam, your PSA came back very high. It's gone from a 0 to a 7. I don't understand. I want to run the test again just to make sure, though the lab rarely misses." With heart sinking, Sam underwent the test again and shuffled home to tell his wife the bad news. A couple of long days ensued.

"On a Friday evening, as we talked about the doctor's findings and dawdled over dinner," Sam recounted, "the phone rang. I got up from the table and absent-mindedly answered it." It was his doctor.

"Sam, I just got the results back from your second PSA. You're fine. No problem. You registered 0. The lab did make a mistake. Don't know if they ran your first test wrong or if they got yours mixed up with another man's. No matter. You're fine. I apologize for the anxiety this has caused you and your family. See you in six months."

"The good news from the doctor caused me to think about a visit from a hospital chaplain I received while I was recovering," Sam told me. "The young man came by my room. Stood at the foot of my bed, as far as he could get from me as possible. Must have thought I was contagious. Chatted. Had a short prayer and turned to leave, saying, 'I'll come back if the Lord wills.'"

With his infectious laugh, Sam recalled, "The chaplain did not come back. Guess it was not the Lord's will for me to get a second visit." He paused a moment, then added, "But I guess it was the Lord's will for me to beat prostate cancer."

Nelson's Story

For many years, Nelson's was a regular face on television news, earning accolades from his peers and the public for his accurate, capable, often prescient reporting of political events. As age inched up on him, he eased into retirement. He and his wife would play tennis, enjoy the grandchildren, and do more of what they wanted to do.

Since Nelson's family had a history of heart trouble, he always took extra precautions about diet, exercise, and regular checkups. During one of his scheduled physicals, Nelson told his doctor about having to get up in the night to urinate.

"When have you had your PSA checked?" his doctor asked. This time the test registered 5.2. Moderately high but not alarming. The doctor wanted Nelson to return within a few weeks for another PSA. When it registered 7.5, the doctor became alarmed and sent Nelson to a urologist. The TRUS and biopsy revealed prostate cancer. The urologist said, "We've caught it early. I suggest surgery, but I don't believe you'll have any problems after the surgery."

Wanting to be sure, Nelson talked with his daughter, a nurse. She collected articles and other reading materials for her father.

After inquiring around his own city, Nelson decided to go to Johns Hopkins University Hospital in Baltimore, Maryland, for more testing and consultations. Though bone scans and an MRI indicated no spread of the disease, the doctors in the John Walsh group, probably the best-known prostate-cancer team in the country, recommended the radical prostatectomy. They informed Nelson that surgery was a tossup at his age, now sixty-eight. He could have radiation. Or they could simply watch the situation. When Nelson pressed the team, however, they leaned toward surgery, taking into account the lack of prostate cancer in his family and his overall good health. Eventually, Nelson agreed.

When the doctors opened Nelson up, to their dismay they

found the cancer had moved outside the gland and spread to some of his lymph nodes. In this case, they chose not to proceed with surgery.

Nelson and his family were distressed. Would he just have to sit around and wait to die? No. The team assured him that several therapies could slow down the disease—if not put it completely in remission.

Then a breakthrough came. One of the doctors on his consultation team urged a certain type of beam radiation. Later, Nelson learned that others on the team were not sure this protocol would have any effect at all. The location of Nelson's cancer seemed to work against beam radiation. But the oncologist disagreed. In fact, he believed the specific location of Nelson's problems would lend itself well to a new technique. Nelson and the team agreed it was worth a try.

The radiation approach called for thirty-nine treatments. Nelson and his wife would have to drive from the Washington, D.C., area to Baltimore, about an hour's drive, for thirty-nine exposures to the beam machine.

Nelson jokes, "The positive part of the process was that we discovered some delightful places to eat lunch in greater Baltimore during that long process."

Is he cured today? The doctors will not say. In fact, the medical community will hardly pronounce a cure if the cancer has broken out of the prostate. As an added precaution, he takes a regular treatment of Lupron, a hormone that supports the beam-radiation treatment. He continues to go for regular checkups, but so far the doctors have seen no sign of a return of the cancer. They hold out much hope for Nelson and his wife.

"I could not ask for more than that," he says confidently.

Coming Back

We all celebrate the fact that we live, that we have survived prostate cancer. Regardless of the lingering effects, the differing degrees of disability and/or inconvenience, we have survived to tell our stories. Unfortunately, many men do not make it this far. They have already been "gathered to their fathers," as the Bible puts it.

Life, despite its ups and downs, is sweet. In the early morning as I pad down the driveway to get the newspaper, I look about me. I breathe the good air. I hear birds singing, maybe now a bit more clearly than I used to. Rain does not matter much. If I get caught in it, I only scurry a bit faster. I take greater delight in my wife, church, grandchildren, and friends. By the grace of God, I am alive.

> **We all celebrate the fact that we live, that we have survived prostate cancer.**

My fellow survivors and I readily admit to the inconvenience of the occasionally leaky plumbing. Most, I am glad to report, fall into the "practically no problems" category.

Sexual activity also moves along the continuum with as much variety as stories told. One colleague declares he had full sex complete with an erection a few weeks after surgery. Bless him. Most, however, report a less dramatic restoration. But they do report some reinvigoration. One of the men gave a particularly helpful word: "Certainly the 'old-fashioned way' is best, but it is not the only way." And advances continue to be made in helping men regain sexual satisfaction, with the pump and an injection being the two most popular assists.

Resumption of full sexual activity takes time. Good relations going into the surgery help couples weather the new realities better. Sometimes the exigencies of the surgery bring a couple closer despite the pre-existing condition of the relationship.

If any problems from the surgery persist, see you doctor or counselor. Do not suffer in silence.

These few years down the road from my surgery, my urologist still wants me to keep a regular check on my PSA level. I go to my primary-care physician, Dr. Corson, every three months for the test. She then sends a copy of the results to Dr. Regan. At my last visit to Dr. Regan's office, he told me I need not return to him for a year, probably because he knows Dr. Corson sees me regularly. He also urged me to call him if anything out of the ordinary occurs.

How do I feel about myself?

I feel altered. I miss aspects of my personal life. I am grateful for good care. Still, as is my natural bent, I move on with optimism and energy.

Conclusion

If you take nothing else from this book, take this: Get tested regularly. Begin at age forty, especially if you find yourself in that category of men at high risk or with a history of prostate cancer in the family. Only by knowing the facts of your own situation can you and your doctor make wise determinations.

In all likelihood, my family and I would still have the pleasure of my father's company if he had not let prostate cancer get away from him. By the grace of God I will see my grandsons, Will, Jake, and Luke, graduate from high school, maybe even college. Who knows, I might even get to escort their grandmother down the church aisle for their weddings. Hey, the scamps might even invite me to say a few carefully crafted words over them and their chosen ones. I do not believe I would embarrass them too much by blubbering just a bit while I gave them my blessing.

If I did drop a few tears, they could excuse me with a wave of the hand and an aside to their young friends, "Hey, what can you expect from an old preacher like that?"

Appendix:
What Wives Need to Know

When I was growing up in Georgia, my mother would gather my two brothers and me, any cousins who might be visiting, and even neighborhood children around the kitchen table and tell us stories about the Bible and about our family. I can't remember the first time I heard the story of how my wily but illiterate Papa Cook hired someone to write love letters to Granny, hoping to sweet talk her into becoming his wife. She finally agreed to marry him, then nearly left him when she found out he could neither read nor write. Despite that rocky beginning, they managed to stay together nearly sixty years, bring ten children into the world, and rear them on a small farm near the deep south Georgia "metropolis" of Whigham. This story and many more became part and parcel of who I am.

When Bob and I had our children, we, too, gathered them together and told them those same stories and many more, including the time in the 1870s when members of a native Creek tribe came swooping on horseback into the tiny village of Roanoke, Alabama, snatched away Bob's Great-grandmother Manley, then a babe-in-arms, and galloped out of sight. Fortunately, in a few minutes they came roaring back with the screaming baby and plopped her into her mother's trembling arms!

These and other stories are so familiar that one family member suggested giving all our sagas a number so we could save the time of telling again the actual tale. We could simply say, "Remember story #11?" or "Oh, yeah, joke #36 would fit that," or

"What about tale #212?" Everybody would respond with the appropriate sigh or giggle.

The book you have been reading is my husband's story dealing with prostate cancer. Bob has told you with humor and candor about the episode, what he learned from it, and what you should know. But prostate cancer is not just a man's story; it is a family story, actually involving everyone connected to that man. I hope that Bob and I will live long enough to sit around the dining-room table and tell this story to our grandchildren and their spouses and their children so often that someone will suggest we assign it a number. Admittedly, a story about cancer isn't what you think of when you pass on family lore, yet this is worth talking about if it saves one person's life or helps deal with the stresses in a marriage.

Bad News

My husband, Bob, is one of four boys. I was the first female, other than his mother, to invade the household. His father made me feel like a princess with his jokes, antics, and general outpouring of love. From the beginning of my connection with the Maddoxes, the experience was fun and exhilarating—love and laughter at its best.

In 1970 Daddy Maddox entered the hospital for prostate surgery after, unbeknownst to Bob and me, "watchfully waiting" on a lump in his prostate for two years. I was sitting on Daddy Maddox's hospital bed, talking and laughing, when the doctor came in after his operation and told him his tumor had been inoperable. Seven years of treatment and recurrence followed.

To the end, Daddy maintained a good sense of humor and an inspiring faith. We drew strength from him but also enjoyed our time together. We grieved at his death and still miss him. We especially grieve at the time wasted "watching" such a lethal invasion of his body.

Years later, I did not do much more than agree when Bob told me, "I think I will go see Dr. Regan. I don't want to take any chances of a repeat of Daddy's performance." Bob went to the doctor and came home to say, "I have a problem. Dr. Regan found a growth on my prostate. He believes it is cancer." You know the rest of the story.

My reaction was the same as the one that day in Daddy Maddox's hospital room: This was definitely bad news. My mind raced one minute to hoping for the best, the next minute to fearing the worst. The possibility of Bob's death filled my soul with fear.

Good News

At dawn on a Wednesday in late May, 1994, we went to the hospital for Bob's surgery. Through the long hours, I sat with family, friends, and fellow church members. I was scared. I wanted to cry. I even wanted to run away.

When Dr. Regan came out of the operating room to tell me that the cancer was contained and they had been able to remove it with surgery, I was vastly relieved. Still, my mind played tricks on me. Is the worst yet to come? What if the doctor is wrong? What if the pathologist comes back with a grim report? Could there be more cancer lurking in his body?

As I visited with Bob, tended to him in the hospital, and then brought him home, my fears were not alleviated. I thought he looked pale. Any pain he mentioned panicked me. "Don't you need to call the doctor? You should at least talk to the nurse!" I buzzed anxiously. Despite my fears, however, Bob recuperated. As he has described, he responded well at every turn. His attitude, the skill of the doctors, and the care of the medical staff combined to make a positive experience of this negative situation.

Bob amazed us all with his determination to follow the doctor's orders. If he was told to stay in for four weeks, that is precisely what he did, despite the fact that he had never even stayed home for four days due to illness before. If he was told that such and such was to happen in one month, that's what happened. He refused to allow any negative thoughts from me, the family, or well-wishers pull at his positive attitude. He had read extensively about prostate cancer, but he did not fall into the trap of deciding the possible negative side effects would cripple him.

In time, I realized that my fears were diminishing. Bob was

going to live through this bout with prostate cancer. That was the good news. Little else mattered as long as he had his life. In talking with the wives of other men who have faced this cancer, I learned that their reactions were similar to mine. We all were so grateful for life the negative side effects of the surgery were swept under the rug.

Two Side Effects No One Wants to Talk About

The two most common lingering results of radical prostatectomy are incontinence and impotence. Bob has already discussed these in the book. What I want to do is talk about these two problems from the woman's point of view, because both, to varying degrees, bear on the relationship between husband and wife. Even as I write about these two conditions, I feel a measure of guilt. With my husband alive and doing very well, what right do I have even to think about the lingering problems? Am I ungrateful? No. I am human; I have my own feelings; I live with ongoing hopes and dreams for our remaining years, and I do not want any unnecessary interference.

One day my daughter-in-law Tina, who delights and amazes us with her openness, had a brief conversation with me about the side effects of the cancer. She mentioned some information she had read. I kept those thoughts in the back of my mind wondering what other women in my situation thought or did.

As time moved along, I began systematically researching how the wives of other prostate cancer survivors had handled these side effects. Most often, I found that the women failed to deal forthrightly with these two "elephants in the living room." They just tried to ignore them.

I talked with many women, sometimes in prearranged meetings over coffee, at other times by coincidence. They ranged from fifty to seventy years of age, and they all told me their stories. For the most part, surgery had occurred from one to five years prior to our talks. Always, I found the women willing but cautious to talk about it.

Their reactions were varied: Some wives chose to move to

another bedroom using the "he needs more space, more comfort" line. Some wives quietly went away, literally moving out after this, the final straw in a bad marriage. (This was, however, not the norm.) Some wives met the challenge head on, making extra time for their husbands, and even going out of town to be together early on.

I came away from these conversations with one overriding conclusion: *The common experience these women shared was of a lack of communication about the surgery and its side effects.* Wives, husbands, and families did not talk much about the surgery, much less the "elephants" hanging about in the living room—the "elephants" of incontinence and impotence. Furthermore, in my view, the medical community, perhaps not wanting to paint the worst scenario, failed to take sufficient time to explain the possibilities and implications of these lingering effects. To be sure, these topics do not enhance a dinner party. But the fact of the matter is that if we're going to deal openly and honestly with the leftovers from prostate cancer, we have to talk about these conditions.

Incontinence. Thankfully, our family has developed a propensity to talk with a refreshing measure of openness about many problems. On the heels of his surgery, Bob took ownership, you might say, of his incontinence. We were able to talk, even laugh, with Bob about this problem. For instance, Bob, following the doctor's orders, did not drive after the surgery for four weeks. During that time, he sent any family member or close friend— whoever happened to be handy in his hour of need—to the drug store for his bag of Depends. Each one dispatched on the errand came back laughing, hoping that the store clerk would not think "it" was for him or her. Also, Bob had very specific requirements which sometimes sent us from store to store. We thank God that we could laugh and say, "How long will this last?"

Bob was so devoted to the doctor's forecast, that if the doctor had said this side effect would be gone in four months, we would have been able to count the days. It also helped that we knew the details and could encourage him as his condition improved and the time drew near to take whatever next steps were suggested.

Even these brief comments here will make some people uncomfortable. While they are relatively easy for me to discuss, other wives I interviewed asked, "How are you going to talk about incontinence in a book?!" I admitted I was not sure, but I told the wives that it is so important that communication take place, I had to try. All the women said their husbands had some measure of incontinence. It is so common, to some degree, among prostate cancer survivors that neither men nor women make a big deal about it.

Impotence. If you think incontinence makes for bad dinner-table conversation, try impotence. As aggravating as chronic incontinence is for men, persistent impotence is even worse. Yet we, both men and women, need not feel isolated in this. The problem of impotence and the impairment of sexual intimacy are painful and difficult to talk about, but ignoring them is far more detrimental.

Working through the problem of impotence is difficult. The varying reactions to this post-operative problem relates directly to what has previously occurred in the marriage. The relationship prior to surgery directly affects, but does not have to determine, the outcome. I think the bottom line answer lies in communication between the husband and wife. The better the communication, the greater the possibility for strengthening the future of the relationship.

"Help is on the way if you seek it."

"You are not alone."

"You can work out the problems."

All these comments, often made through tears and laughter, come from people who have, in one way or another, made their own good news. The oft-spoken word that needs to be emphasized for us all faced with impotence is that *intimacy does not have to suffer because of the reduction or loss of physical ability.* We all have a need, a craving for the measure of intimacy that is possible only between husband and wife. The spouses each have physical, sexual, and emotional needs that only each other can meet. It is not necessary to deny these needs because of an impairment. So where do you go for help?

First, you should have a conversation with your husband's doctor. New medical protocols seem to be emerging regularly that can provide physical assistance for overcoming impotence.

Beyond the medical community, however, you should look to each other. It is extremely important to realize that there are many steps to building, rebuilding, strengthening, and enhancing the relationship while coming up with ways to circumvent any physical problems brought on by the operation. Both of you want to avoid hurting the husband, since he has already suffered trauma to his mind and body from the surgery. And, you both should want to support the wife who has enjoyed the intimate relationship in the past. Together, you must face the new realities that have entered your lives. Assure each other of your love and desire to move towards greater intimacy.

The feelings that first drew you as a couple together can form the foundation of your new relationship. Reclaim these feelings, and rediscover the fun things you loved to do together before making a living and raising the kids pushed those fun things out of your lives. Reaffirm your love for each other and make each other feel secure in that renewed commitment. Look for new ways to express love, and try to become ever more open and vulnerable to each other.

You will find that this process of moving forward in your intimate relationship is very time consuming. Don't be discouraged! It takes thought, communication, and a willingness to understand and be understood. This process calls for you to nurture one another while trying to avoid putting pressure on each other. It is not an easy task, but it can be accomplished with prayer, openness, and persistence.

Frankly, I do not have a story of a couple who have returned to the exact physical level they enjoyed prior to prostate surgery. I am sure such couples exist, and I would like to hear their stories. But I realize that this topic does not lend itself to a great deal of "Let me tell you what happened to us . . . ." Consequently, there are many stories I have not heard.

I do, however, have many stories of couples who have found a new level of intimacy. They now are able to communicate with greater freedom; they can love each other physically, albeit dif-